Aircraft of the
US AIR FORCE
AND ITS NATO ALLIES

Aircraft of the
US AIR FORCE
AND ITS NATO ALLIES

Edited by Bill Yenne

GALLERY BOOKS
An imprint of W.H. Smith Publishers Inc.
112 Madison Avenue
New York, New York 10016

A Bison Book

Published by Gallery Books
A Division of W H Smith Publishers Inc.
112 Madison Avenue
New York, New York 10016

Produced by
Bison Books Corp.
15 Sherwood Place
Greenwich, CT 06830

β-C.2
Q
358.43
A

ISBN 0-8317-0195-1

Printed in Hong Kong

1 2 3 4 5 6 7 8 9 10

Page 1: A US Air Force Fairchild A-10 Thunderbolt of the 81st Tactical Fighter Wing, based at Bentwaters-Woodbridge in the United Kingdom, lands at Det-1 at Sembach, West Germany.

Pages 2-3: Three McDonnell Douglas F-15 Eagles do rollout maneuvers over a European cloud cover. Their CR tail coding indicates that they are based at the US Air Forces in Europe (USAFE) air base, Camp New Amsterdam, at Soesterberg in the Netherlands.

These pages: The Boeing E-3 Sentry is an AWACS (Airborne Warning and Control System) aircraft, loaded with computers and electronic sensing devices. In the event of war, E-3s like this one would assume the role of airborne battle management centers, directing the movements of many of NATO's fighters and attack aircraft.

The palindromic legend surrounding the compass rose on this Sentry includes the North Atlantic alliance's acronym in both English (NATO) and French (OTAN). The NATO/OTAN Sentrys have since been repainted with the Luxembourg national crest.

CONTENTS

NATO ✦ OTAN

CHAPTER 1

An Overview of NATO History

by Bill Yenne

If a Third World War is ever fought with conventional weapons, it is likely that central Europe will be its center stage. If that war comes, air superiority over the battlefields of central Europe will mean the difference between winning and losing. In the meantime, the quality of NATO airpower stands as a major deterrent in preventing the Third World War.

This is a book about the United States Air Forces in Europe, the NATO Alliance and the air defense of western Europe, but more than any of these, it is a book about World War III. Some say that the third world war *started* before the second one ended, but *certainly* the seeds were sown in the rubble of the second. If and when it comes, that third global conflict will start in very nearly the same place as the first two, on that ambiguous but not imaginary dividing line between what we perceive as eastern and western Europe.

On 26 June 1945, midway between the surrenders of Nazi Germany and Imperial Japan in May and September, representatives of 50 nations met in San Francisco to sign the United Nations Charter. As soon as Japan was defeated and

the final surrender signed in September 1945, the United States and Great Britain began a rapid demobilization. The war had ended and it seemed that peace had been won.

Meeting at the Potsdam Conference in July 1945, US President Harry Truman, Soviet Premier Josef Stalin and British Prime Minister Clement Attlee(who replaced Winston Churchill in the midst of the conference) decided on the postwar shape of Europe. The plan was to prevent future war and because Germany had initiated two world wars in less than half a century, it was sliced up into four occupation zones that would be administered by Britain, France, the United States and the Soviet Union. These zones would keep Germany too small to threaten the peace and recovery that the western Allies planned for *all* of Europe.

Within a matter of months, however, it became clear that a new threat had emerged from the very heart of the Grand Alliance that had defeated Germany. This new threat emerged out of the East and cast its shadow across Europe. When Germany surrendered, the United States and Britain had roughly five

Left, from left: Looking like the cat who ate the canary, Soviet dictator Josef Stalin poses with his soon-to-be betrayed allies, US President Franklin D Roosevelt and British Prime Minister Winston Churchill.

Above: The placard on the truck proclaims the millionth ton of Marshall Plan aid to arrive in Greece, in December of 1949. The Marshall Plan was President Truman's strategy for the containment of communism by materially aiding disadvantaged European countries.

Airpower of the fallen Reich: An infantryman of the US Seventh Army's 63rd Infantry Division (*opposite*) checks one of a pair of captured Messerschmitt Me-262 jet fighters in April of 1945. The Luftwaffe's jets were much more advanced than those of the Allies and made it into service earlier.

million combat personnel in Europe, while the Soviet Union had six million. A year later, the two Western Allies had reduced their personnel levels to 880,000, while the Soviets had yet to demobilize. With Nazi Germany lying in ruin and defeat, the vast armed might of the Red Army turned its attention to the subjugation of the people of eastern Europe and the intimidation of the people of western Europe.

Even before the end of the war, the Soviet Union had annexed the nations of Estonia, Latvia and Lithuania, as well as portions of Czechoslovakia, Finland, Germany, Poland and Romania. As the Red Army pushed the German Army out of Romania, Poland, Hungary and Czechoslovakia, the political commissars followed closely behind, recruiting local communists to rule the recaptured lands, putting them into power and keeping them in power through the armed force of the Red Army.

The Soviets refused to permit the promised free elections in Poland and refused their allies access to the eastern zone of Germany. Winston Churchill, Britain's wartime prime minister, spoke of an 'Iron Curtain' descending across Europe and deplored the fact that the West did not know what was going on behind it. What *was* going on soon came into chilling clarity: the Soviet Union was turning eastern Europe into a buffer zone of dependent satellite nations. Democratic governments that asserted themselves were subverted, and by 1948 communist parties were the ruling party in every country that the Red Army had occupied after the war.

In June 1947, American Secretary of State George Marshall instituted the 'Marshall Plan' for postwar European recovery. Calling the Marshall Plan 'an instrument of American Imperialism,' Soviet dictator Josef Stalin, in September 1947, set up the Cominform, an institution designed to subvert the Marshall Plan and strengthen Soviet domination of the eastern European communist parties.

Czechoslovakia, a democracy born in 1918 out of the ruins of the Austro-Hungarian Empire, was occupied and dominated by Nazi Germany from 1938 to 1945. In October 1945, six months after World War II, the Czechs reinstituted their democratic form of government with a provisional National Assembly selecting Dr Edward Benes as president. In 1947, the Czech cabinet approved the participation of Czechoslovakia in the Marshall Plan. Soviet agents within the county immediately undertook to foment unrest inside the little central European republic. In February 1948, the local communist party—with Soviet support—seized control of the govern-

General of the Army George Marshall (*right, at right*) says 'until we meet again' to his successor as Army Chief of Staff, Dwight D Eisenhower. In this 1945 photo, Marshall departs the western world to fulfill his new post as ambassador to China. Later, as US Secretary of State, Marshall was responsible for the 'Marshall Plan' for the recovery of Europe.

Opposite: A US Army C-54 transport is shown being loaded in West Germany with staple goods for the people of West Berlin, during the Berlin Airlift of 1947-1949, which was dubbed 'Operation Vittles' by US pilots flying the missions.

ment. President Benes was forced to resign and Foreign Minister Jan Masaryk, son of the country's first president, committed 'suicide' under suspicious circumstances, and was found dead on the sidewalk in front of his home where he had 'fallen.'

On 4 March 1948, six days before Mr Masaryk's death, representatives of Britain and France met in Brussels with representatives of Belgium, Luxembourg and the Netherlands to discuss a mutual assistance treaty. This agreement, the Brussels Treaty of 17 March 1948, was dedicated to common defense against 'armed aggression in Europe' in which the five nations would render 'all the military aid and assistance in their power' in the defense of any of their members attacked by a hostile outside power. This organization, known as the 'Western Union' or 'Consultative Council,' was the first true precursor to NATO.

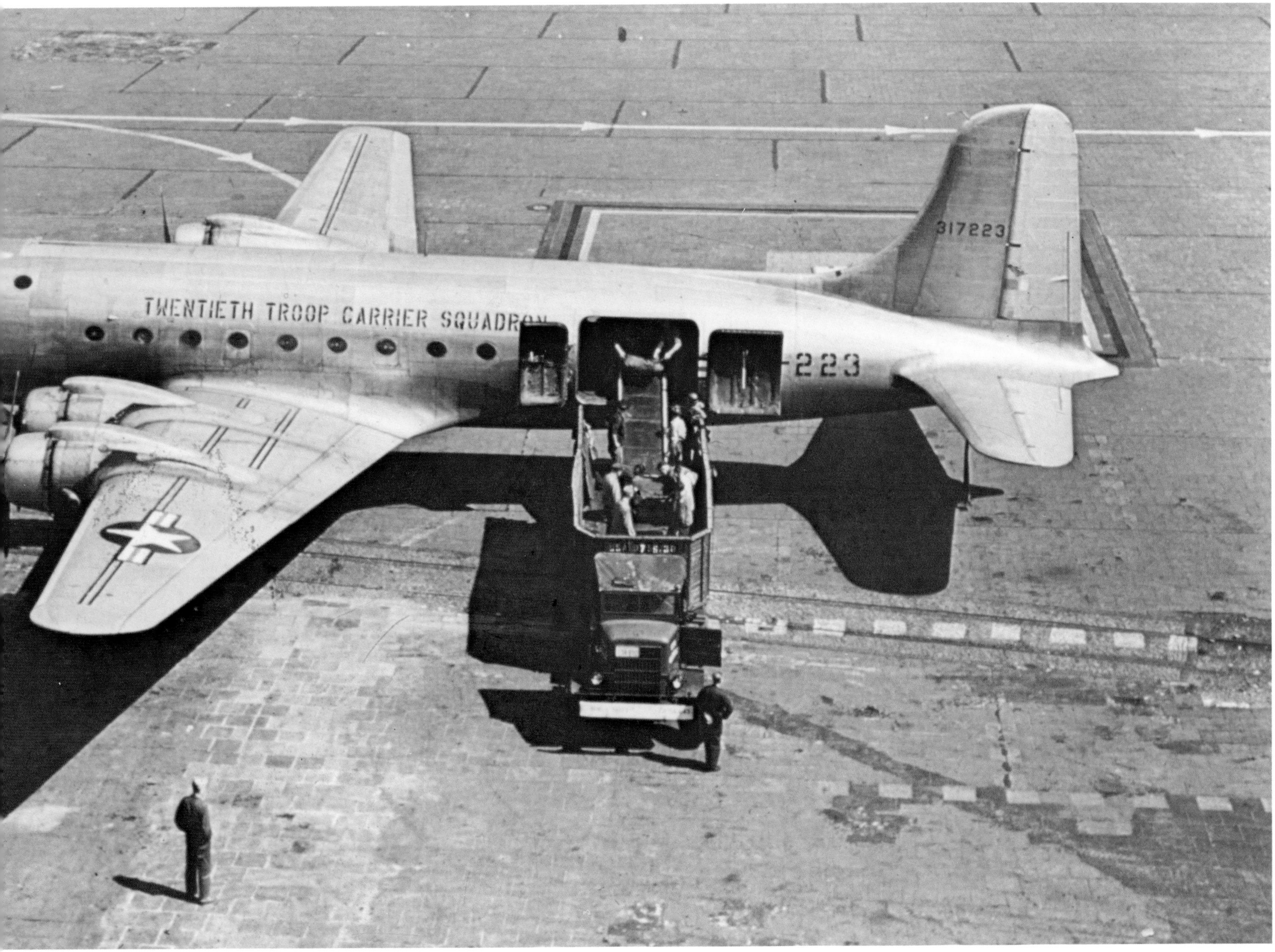
TWENTIETH TROOP CARRIER SQUADRON
317223
223

On 30 April, the Defense Ministers and Chiefs of Staff of these five signatories met in London to discuss specific military requirements. This organizational level of the five-nation alliance, known as the Western Defence Committee, was joined by observers from the United States and Canada in July.

In June 1948, however, the Soviet Union made its own move into the context of European power politics. Berlin, capital of prewar Germany, was divided into four zones like the rest of Germany. Berlin was in the heart of the Soviet zone, but a four-power agreement guaranteed Britain, France and the United States access to their respective zones via road and rail routes *through* the Soviet zone. On 24 June, Soviet troops suddenly sealed off these routes, blockading Berlin. The Soviet move was designed to force its former allies to abandon their zones in the former Nazi capital. The Russians knew that the British and American armies, gutted by demobilization, could not challenge the Red Army to break the blockade overland, but they failed to take into account the possibility that the western Allies would simply *fly over* the blockaded land routes.

It was a massive undertaking, but the challenge had to be met. General Curtis LeMay, commander of the US Air Forces in Europe (USAFE) immediately organized an airlift using the C-47 and C-54 transports that he had available under his command. President Harry Truman decided that the United States should take on the responsibility of supplying the entire population of the beleaguered city for as long as the blockade might last. The US Air Force's Military Air Transport Service (MATS) quickly sent in planes to augment the initial USAFE effort, as did Britain's Royal Air Force (RAF).

MATS General William Tunner, who had managed the airlift of supplies across the Himalayas into China during World War II, took charge of the Berlin Airlift, now codenamed Operation Vittles. He brought together US Air Force transports—C-47 Skytrains, C-54 Skymasters and C-82 Packets—from all over the world. He supplemented these with US Navy R5Ds (the Navy equivalent of the C-54) from the Naval Air Transport Service (NATS) and contracted for American commercial airlines to airlift supplies to Europe, where they would be picked up by his military transports for the last haul into Berlin.

Tunner's Combined Airlift Task Force (CALTF) set up a 24-hour-a-day aerial bridge between Weisbaden and Frankfurt in western Germany and Berlin in the east. By July, the CALTF transports were landing in Berlin every third minute, carrying

Opposite page: US Army C-54s are being unloaded at Tempelhof Air Base in West Berlin, during the Airlift. *Above:* The 'Jack of All Trades' Republic F-84 Thunderstreak, with some of its tools. The F-84 served with a number of NATO air forces including those of the United States and West Germany.

everything from livestock to coal. Through the bitter winter of 1948–49, they flew through rain, snow, sleet and fog: 150,000 sorties delivering 2,325,000 tons of supplies. On 12 May 1949, the Soviets finally admitted defeat and discontinued their blockade. The aircraft of the US Air Force and the nations that would soon be its NATO allies had met the first challenge put up by the Soviets and they had won!

In the meantime, western Europe had come to realize what Churchill had meant by an Iron Curtain having been drawn across Europe from the Baltic to the Balkans.

In September 1948, a military body had been established within the context of the 17 March Brussels Treaty. Britain's wartime hero, Field Marshal Bernard Montgomery, was named Chairman and headquarters were established at Fontainebleau, France. Other Commanders included France's General de Lattre de Tassigny for land forces, Britain's Air Chief Marshal Sir James Robb for air forces and France's Vice Admiral Jaujard for naval forces.

In October 1948, the Brussels Treaty signatories and representatives of the United States and Canada jointly announced that they had reached 'complete identity of views on the principle of a defensive pact for the North Atlantic area.' These parties in turn invited Denmark, Iceland, Italy, Norway and Portugal to join them in a mutual aid treaty covering North Atlantic security. Despite outright Soviet threats against these 12 western nations, the North Atlantic Treaty was signed on 4 April 1949 at Washington DC. The North Atlantic Treaty Organization (NATO) was born.

The North Atlantic Council had first taken up the notion of West German participation in NATO's integrated defense in September 1950, when it was recognized that its soil would be the first battlefield in any potential conflict. There was long-term reluctance to accede to a rearmament of Germany, because the German role in World War II was still fresh in everyone's mind.

In December 1950, the North Atlantic Council approved its Defense Committee's recommendation for the creation of a single centralized, multinational military command, unified under a single commander. This command would be designated as the Allied Command Europe (ACE) and its Commander as the Supreme Allied Commander for Europe (SACEUR). As its first SACEUR, the Atlantic Council picked US Army five-star General Dwight David Eisenhower, who had served as the Supreme Allied Commander in the European theater during World War II, as Chief of Staff of the US

Opposite page: The venerable C-47 Skytrain, aka the 'Gooney Bird,' the World War II workhorse that also served so well in the Berlin Airlift alongside the more capacious C-54. The Skytrain, a *very* tough plane, lived on into the years of the Vietnam War, in which the C-47 became the high-intensity AC-47 'Spooky' gunship.

Above: Mechanics overhaul a Gloster Meteor F.4 of the RAF's 66th Squadron at Duxford in 1949. An earlier model Meteor, the F.3, was the first Allied jet fighter to see service—as of July 1944, during World War II.

Army from November 1945 through 1948, and as president of Columbia University until recalled into uniform to command NATO's fledgling military forces.

Eisenhower's headquarters, which were designated as Supreme Headquarters, Allied Powers Europe (SHAPE), were established at Rocquencourt near Paris, France on 2 April 1951. Since 1952, when Eisenhower retired to run successfully for the American presidency, the post of SACEUR has been held by a four-star US Army General. The parallel post of Supreme Allied Commander for the Atlantic (SACLANT) was established in January 1952 and has always been held by a US Navy admiral. A third and coequal NATO post, that of Allied Commander in Chief for the English Channel/Pas de Calais, was established the following month and has always been held by an admiral of the British Royal Navy.

In February 1952, Greece and Turkey formally joined NATO, followed in turn by the Federal Republic of (West)

Opposite page: Stones against tanks: Oppressed East German youths stone Soviet T-34 tanks on the streets of Berlin during June of 1953.

Above: A Douglas DC-4 (the commercial version of the C-54) of Belgium's postwar national airline. Commercial Air transport also played a crucial role in helping to re-establish the national identity of the European nations which were ravaged by the war.

At left: President Eisenhower is shown here during a visit to the SHAPE headquarters in 1959. To President Eisenhower's *left* is the Supreme Allied Commander at the time, General Lauris Norstad.

Germany in May 1955 and by Spain in May 1982. In 1967, French President Charles de Gaulle formally withdrew his country from NATO's military command. France, however, continued to be part of NATO politically.

On 14 May 1955, the Soviet Union reacted to Germany's entry into NATO nine days prior by organizing its own parallel military organization—the Warsaw Pact—containing all of its eastern European satellites. The following year, in October 1956, a popular anticommunist revolution erupted in Hungary in response to the harsh economic conditions imposed on Hungary since the early 1950s. The communists asked former Premier Imre Nagy to set up a coalition government to restore order. Nagy decided to declare Hungary a neutral country and withdrew the nation from the Warsaw Pact. It was the first and only time that any country dared such a move. Within a matter of days, Nagy was deposed by one of his ministers, Janos Kadar, who called in Soviet tanks to put down the rebellion. Nagy was executed and the Warsaw Pact had its bloody baptism of fire.

NATO'S EARLY AIRPOWER

When NATO was born in 1949, its combat aircraft assets were a pitiful shadow of what had existed just four years before. When the US Army Air Forces became the independent US Air Force in September 1947, it inherited an aircraft strength that was less than a third of the USAAF peak—and falling. Personnel levels had dropped to barely more than 12 percent of the wartime peak, with a parallel and devastating loss of qualified pilots. The British Royal Air Force (RAF) had, meanwhile, undergone a similar scaling down.

The cornerstone of the US Air Force contribution to NATO was the US Air Forces in Europe (USAFE), which had been established in August 1947 around the remnants of the VIII Fighter Command, the fighter organization of the USAAF Eighth Air Force. During World War II, the Eighth Air Force had become one of the largest components of the USAAF, with the principal task of carrying out the aerial bombardment of Nazi-held Europe from bases in England. The Eighth had been composed of an VIII Bomber Command, which managed its B-17 and B-24 heavy bombers, and an VIII Fighter Command, which managed the fighter escorts for the VIII Bomber Command.

After the defeat of Nazi Germany, the Eighth Air Force and its VIII Bomber Command were moved to the Pacific where

Opposite page: Seen here in its wartime glory circa 1944, the P-51D Mustang was an important element of the USAFE contribution to NATO's early airpower five years later. The Mustang was an excellent fighter/fighter bomber and attack plane in both World War II and the Korean War, and served as a reconnaissance plane for years after.

The P-51 Mustang was the backbone of the VIII Fighter Command during World War II, and after the war many of them were left behind in Europe. The Mustang, a handsome plane with 37 foot wingspan, was equipped at first with an 1150 hp Allison engine, which some pilots swore by, claiming their 'little horsey' handled better with that engine than with the later, more powerful (1680 hp) Merlin engines.

Arms included four .50 caliber machine guns (variants were .30 caliber mg's), rockets and provision for 1000 pounds of bombs.

Mustangs were redesignated as F-51D in 1948, and they also were repainted with red sidebars in the national insignia.

At right, Royal Air Force Gloster Meteor T-7s fly *en force* above European countryside. T-7s were the trainer versions of Great Britain's very speedy fighter/reconnaissance jet of the late 1940s and 1950s. Top speed was 598 mph; and a photo recon variant—the PR10—had an operational ceiling of 44,000 feet.

In the early 1950s photo on the *opposite page,* RAF De Havilland Vampire F-3s overfly a patch of British farmland. In 1948, Vampires were the first jet fighters to make an unsupported trans-Atlantic flight. The several series of Vampires used a variety of engines; the DeHavilland Goblin 2, the DH Ghost 2 and the DH Goblin 3—with 3100, 4400 and 3850 pounds of thrust, respectively.

they were intended to help in the final attack on Japan. Having arrived too late for this activity, the Eighth Air Force cycled back to the United States where it was assigned to the new Strategic Air Command (SAC). The VIII Fighter Command, meanwhile, remained in Europe as an element of the forces in the American zone of occupied Germany.

When USAFE was established at the former Luftwaffe base near Weisbaden, the armada of fighter airplanes that had made up the VIII Fighter Command in its heyday just 18–24 months before was only a memory. There were a few P-47 Thunderbolts and P-51 Mustangs scattered on airfields around the zone, and a handful of P-80 Shooting Star jets had begun to make their appearance. By 1949 and 1950, there would be a few F-84 Thunderjets on hand, but when the war in Korea exploded onto the scene in June 1950, the US Air Force had to shift a great deal of its attention to this threat.

The postwar RAF was armed with later marks of the Supermarine Spitfire, a plane whose earlier marks had been Britain's first line of defense during the Battle of Britain six years before. The venerable Spits were supplemented by other piston-engined fighters that had been brought on line toward the end of the war, such as Hawker's Tempest, Typhoon and Fury. Meanwhile, Britain's first jet fighter, the Gloster Meteor, which had appeared in limited numbers before the war ended, was now available as the RAF's front line fighter until more advanced types, such as the Hawker Hunter, made their debut in the early 1950s.

Strategic bombers played little role in NATO or its precursors, although the RAF Bomber Command (Strike Command after 1968) and the US Air Force Strategic Air Command

continued on page 26

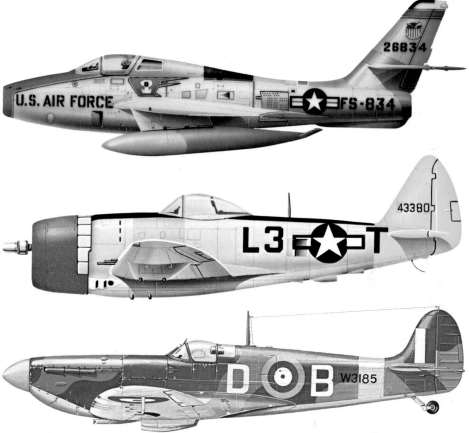

Early NATO airpower included its member nations' first generation jet fighters, such as the Lockheed F-80 (*left*) and the Republic F-84 Thunderflash (*top*), as well as the World War II-vintage Republic Thunderbolt (*above, middle*) and Supermarine Spitfire (*above*).

Aircraft such as the P-47 (F-47 after 1948) that survived the war, formed the backbone of the much reduced American VIII Fighter Command as it became a component of USAFE and in turn a component of NATO. This Republic Aircraft company creation could cruise at 300 mph and fly nearly a thousand miles fully-laden. The company's postwar Thunderstreak could fly half again faster and farther than its not-so-distant ancestor. The F-84 served with the US Air Force and other NATO air forces, including that of the Federal Republic of Germany.

The F-80 Shooting Star, American's first combat jet, made its European debut in 1945 before the war ended, but it did not get into combat. In USAFE's early days, however, it appeared in the skies over Germany in much greater numbers.

The Supermarine Spitfire of the RAF went through a series of improvements during the war, and in postwar years, served as a fighter in the air forces of several European countries, as well as remaining (eventually to be supplanted in this role by the Meteor) a front line fighter and reconnaissance plane for the RAF until April 1954. Spitfire engines ranged from the 1030 hp Merlin II to the 2375 hp Griffon 64. Standard arms were up to eight .303 Browning machine guns, two 20 mm Hispano cannons and in later versions, six to eight three-inch rockets. Spitfires could carry 1000 lbs of bombs.

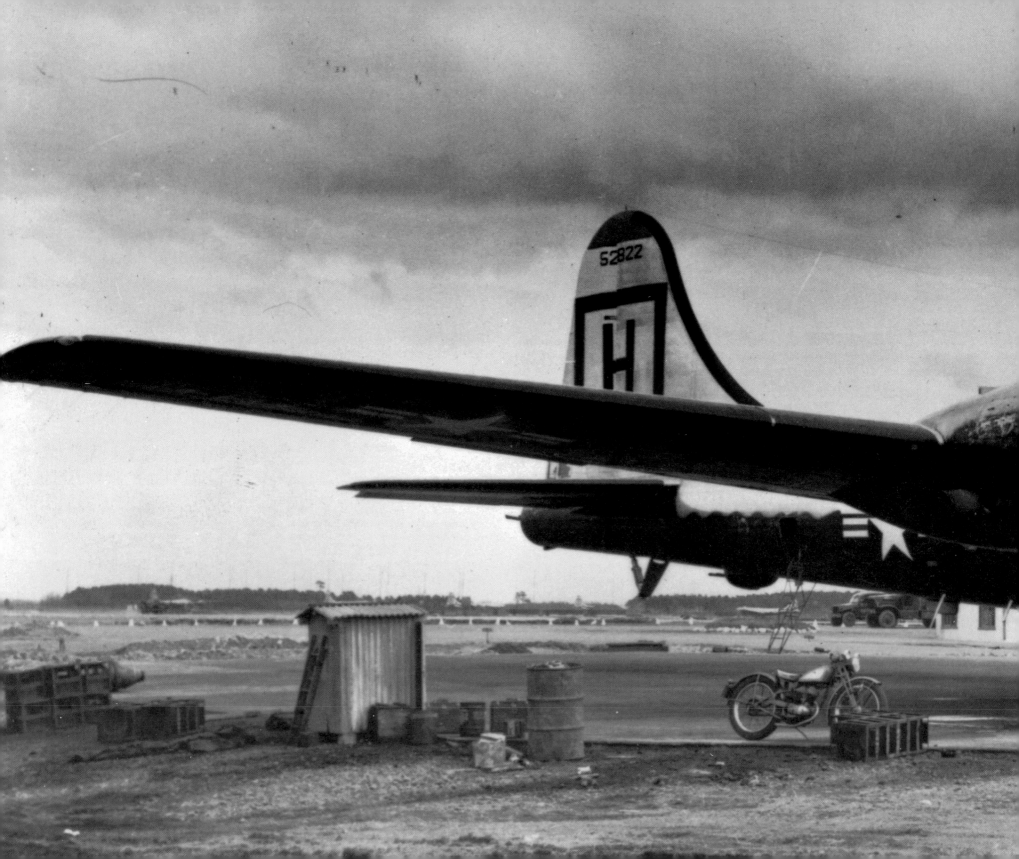

These pages: The truly super B-29 Super-fortress was deployed to Europe as a show of force against Communist aggression. In 1948, during the Berlin Blockade, SAC rotated several of its B-29 squadrons from its 301st Bombardment Group to Furstenfeldbruck Air Base in Germany and the RAF fields at Marham and Waddington in England.

A V Roe's war era Lancaster heavy bomber (*below right*) begat the postwar Lincoln which was similar in overall configuration, and entered service in September 1945. Lincoln squadrons were detached to Singapore after World War II in an antiterrorist campaign against communist insurgents. Lincolns were withdrawn from first-line service with the RAF in September of 1955. The Lancaster/Lincoln design also gave birth (in 1949) to the Avro Shackleton, a variant of which still serves the RAF as an Airborne Early Warning (AEW) system.

While the US Air Force Strategic Air Command rotated some of its own B-29s (see the picture *on the previous page* and the text *on this page*) to Europe in the postwar years to rattle a nuclear sabre to back up a fragile NATO, the US also sold a handful to the RAF in 1950.

Designated as Washingtons by the British, the B-29s retained the black-bellied camouflage scheme (see *bottom right*) they'd taken on during their wartime service in the Pacific. The Lincolns, surplus Lancasters and the much more superior Washingtons were the only western European-owned strategic bombers until the British V-bombers arrived on the scene in the early 1950s.

The Russians meanwhile were fussing with stolen B-29s and beginning a line of prop-driven bombers that would start with the Tu-4, which was a direct copy of the B-29, and would reach its apogee in the Tu-20, which is *still* in service.

The Lightning (*opposite*) was the archetypical hot RAF fighter of the 1960s.

(SAC) were (and still are) available to back up NATO in an emergency. In 1945 the RAF Bomber Command and the USAAF Eighth and Fifteenth Air Forces constituted the biggest combined strategic air force in history. By the end of 1946 this force almost had been completely dismantled. Both the Eighth and Fifteenth had moved home and had been assigned to SAC, but most of their B-17s and B-24s had been cut up for scrap. The USAAF Twentieth Air Force in the Pacific—composed entirely of World War II's heaviest bomber, the B-29—was reduced in strength and its B-29s reassigned to SAC in the United States. The great B-29 Superfortress made its operational European debut in November 1946 when six of them were deployed to USAFE's Rhein-Main Air Base near Frankfurt as a show of force after two USAFE C-47s were shot down by communists in Yugoslavia. During the Berlin Blockade in 1948, SAC rotated several B-29 squadrons from its 30lst Bombardment Group to Furstenfeldbruck Air Base in Germany and the RAF fields at Marham and Waddington in England.

When NATO was formed, the air forces of its member nations were composed almost entirely of British and American aircraft types. Surplus World War II types were supplemented in the late 1940s and early 1950s by jets such as the American Republic F-84 series and British Meteors and Hunters.

Until the late 1950s when the former Axis partners, Germany and Italy, got into the act, France was the only other NATO country, aside from Britain and the United States, to develop a first-line combat aircraft industry. Dassault, the firm created immediately after the war by Marcel Bloch, moved ahead with its Ouragan project, which resulted in a trim little straight-winged jet fighter that first flew in February 1949. The Dassault Ouragan was in turn followed by the swept-wing Dassault Mystere series that remained in production until 1959 and in service until the late 1970s.

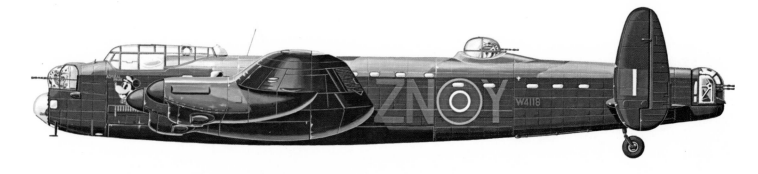

Six Luftwaffe fighter wings flew the Republic F-84F Thunderstreak (*at right*), from 1958-67. The F-84F shown here carries the markings of JBG 34, based at Memmingen, Federal Republic of Germany.

THE ROLE OF GERMANY IN NATO AIRPOWER

In 1967, when French President De Gaulle pulled his country out of NATO's integrated military command, the Federal Republic of Germany took its place as the most important NATO military power on the continent.

Germany as a single, unified nation was born with the proclamation of the German Empire in 1871 and ceased to exist with the collapse of the Third German Reich in 1945. The territory which had comprised pre-1945 Germany was cut up like a pie, and slices of eastern Germany were incorporated into the territory of Poland and the Soviet Union. On the opposite frontier, the Alsace and Lorraine regions, which had bounced back and forth between France and Germany for nearly a century, went back to France. The rest of Germany was divided into four occupation zones. In 1949, Britain, France and the United States agreed to end their occupation and to see those three zones unified into the Federal Republic of Germany. The Soviet Union refused to allow its zone to join this 'new' Germany and established its own Germany in the Soviet zone. This somewhat artificial concoction became the German Democratic Republic, a ready-made, loyal communist ally for the Soviet empire. It was not until the Treaty of Paris in 1955,

however, that the Federal Republic of Germany was allowed to have a national airline or to rebuild its armed forces.

The Federal Republic's air force, the Luftwaffe, was created around a cadre of pilots who had served in the World War II Luftwaffe, and who were now ten years out of practice. During World War II, the German aircraft industry had produced some of the best high-performance airplanes in the world, but these had been destroyed during the war, along with the industry itself. Thus, the new Luftwaffe's first pilots honed their skills in American and British trainers such as the T-33 and the T-6 Texan (British designation: Harvard). The German aircraft industry now also began to struggle to its feet, but it would be a number of years before it was able to produce first-line combat aircraft, so most of the new Luftwaffe's first aircraft were of foreign origin. A majority of the Luftwaffe's first-line fighters were American-built F-84F Thunderstreaks, RF-84F Thunderflashes and F-100D Super Sabres. Also included were F-86K Sabre Jets, which were built by Fiat in Italy under American license. Many of the Luftwaffe's second-line aircraft, however, were foreign types that were domestically produced, such as the Nord Noratlas transport and the Piaggio 149 trainer, that was built by Focke-Wulf.

For bases, the new Luftwaffe found itself in the peculiar po-

The Luftwaffe re-formed in 1955, and was built around a cadre of pilots who had served with the original Luftwaffe in World War II. Since the Federal Republic had no military air industry of its own in the early 1950s, Luftwaffe pilots of this period honed their skills in American and British trainers, and a variety of European training aircraft such as the Fouga CM170R Magister shown *at left*. This particular plane was part of the original French-built batch delivered to FFS-A at Landsberg in 1957.

The Bundesmarine, newly formed in 1956, had no carriers, but sought strike aircraft that could operate from other NATO countries' carriers. But it was not to be—the Armstrong-Whitworth Sea Hawk Mark 100/101s which eventually were flown by Marinefliegergeschwader (MFG) 1 and 2 at Schleswig and Eggebeck until 1964 were land based. *At immediate left:* A Federal Republic Sea Hawk of MFG 2 in the late 1950s.

two ground commands (Kommando der Boden) established at Munster in the north and Karlsruhe in the south to administer airfields and radar sites.

In 1959, as the Luftwaffe matured, the air command groups Luftwaffen Gruppe Nord and Sud were established in Munster and Karlsruhe and attached to NATO's Second and Fourth Allied Tactical Air Forces (ATAF) respectively. Air defense divisions were also established with headquarters at Munster and Munich.

Because of the Federal Republic's position geographically and because of the fact that it directly faces the bulk of the Warsaw Pact forces, the role of the Luftwaffe and its interaction with USAFE and other NATO airpower is the key to allied air superiority over Western Europe in wartime.

NATO COOPERATIVE AIRCRAFT PROGRAMS

One of the first and most important practical problems faced by NATO planners was the standardization of equipment. Such difficulties would not be unexpected when so many sovereign nations join together on a cooperative effort on the scale of NATO. In the case of aircraft, the problem was partially assuaged in the beginning by the use of British and American types. As the years went by, however, the high-tech industrial bases in the other countries recovered from the war and wanted to participate in serious combat aircraft projects. France, of course, both left the NATO military command *and* developed one of the world's most sophisticated aircraft industries, but other countries also had industries which became serious contenders.

There were two ways in which smaller countries could become involved in high-tech aircraft projects without having to develop an aircraft industry to rival Boeing or General Dynamics and these were (A) to build an American-designed or British-designed aircraft under license from the original manufacturer, or (B) to join in an international cooperative effort to produce a single, *multinational* aircraft.

The history of the aircraft industry is filled with examples of the former, and in postwar Europe license production aided in the recovery of national industries and helped pave the way for international programs.

The first multinational aircraft to be developed under NATO auspices was the G-91 Gina, a small, single-engined jet trainer/light attack plane. It was developed in response to a December 1953 NATO specification for a light, multipurpose

Fiat built F-86s and designed the G-91 Gina (*see text,* columns 2-3 *these pages*) light multipurpose strike fighter. The design similarities of the F-86 all-weather fighter and the G-91 are externally striking, and one could almost say that the Gina is a three-quarter size version of the North American F-86 Sabre (*opposite*).

The Gina is a trim 28-feet, one inch (span) by 33-feet, nine inches (length), carries two 30mm cannons and a variety of under-wing ordnance, and tops out at 668 mph. The Gina was manufactured in a single-seater fighter version and a G-91T-1 two-seater training version (*above*).

sition of owning fields that were fewer than, and inferior to, those owned by USAFE in Germany itself! Ironically, these USAFE bases had originally belonged to the *old,* wartime Luftwaffe. The new Luftwaffe's first base at Memmingen was not occupied until October 1956 because the runway had to be lengthened to 7900 feet to bring it up to NATO (and operational jet aircraft) standards. USAFE's Furstenfeldbruck base, which was turned over to the Luftwaffe in November 1956, was soon followed by the USAFE field at Landsberg. Other early bases used by the Luftwaffe were at Buchel, Oldenburg and Erding. The first Luftwaffe combat unit to become operational with the F-84F was the fighter bomber wing (*jagdbomber geschwader*) JBG-31 at Buchal in June 1958.

The early Luftwaffe was divided into five commands: Kommando der Materiel (supplies) based at Erding, Kommando der Schulen (training) based at Furstenfeldbruck, Allgemeine Luftwaffenamt (general headquarters command) at Bonn and

strike-fighter. Loosely based on the American F-86, the G-91 was designed by Fiat in Italy around a British Bristol-Siddeley Orpheus turbojet engine. Originally designed to be in service with the air forces of all of NATO's continental partners, the G-91 initially only served with Italy's Regia Aeronautica and Germany's Luftwaffe, although used Ginas were later transferred to the Greek and Turkish air forces. In fact, there were more G-91s built in Germany than there had been in its native Italy. The respective numbers were 174 and 294, originally, with Messerschmitt, Heinkel and Dornier all involved in the German production. In the mid-1970s, Aeritalia (a consortium of Fiat and Finmeccanica-IRI) built an additional 45 G-91Y aircraft for the Regia Aeronautica.

The most important license production scheme to receive NATO's official imprimatur involved the American Lockheed F-104G Starfighter. The F-104 series had been born in the 1950s out of a Lockheed-initiated design for an ultimate air superiority fighter. The Starfighter was ordered by the US Air Force and made its first flight in 1954, but it achieved most of its notoriety in Europe.

The earlier model Starfighters had been in service with the US Air Force for several years by 1958 when Luftwaffe selected the G-series Starfighter as the centerpiece of its second generation combat aircraft arsenal. In 1959, an agreement was reached whereby the single-seat F-104G (an upgraded version of the single-seat F-104A and F-104C which had been built by Lockheed for the US Air Force) would be produced in Germany by a consortium composed of Dornier, Heinkel, Messerschmitt and Siebel. In the meantime, Canadair had also arranged to produce a variant of the Starfighter, so German and Canadian officials met to discuss standardizing their Starfighters.

Above: **This Canadair Mark 6 Sabre wears the colorful markings of Jagdeschwader 71 'Richtofen.' Sabres were produced by many countries under agreement with North American.**

In March 1960, the governments of both Belgium and the Netherlands decided to acquire the F-104G Starfighter as the centerpiece for *their* air forces. These F-104Gs would be built under Lockheed license by SABCA and Avions Fairey in Belgium, and Fokker in the Netherlands. Italy joined the growing number of NATO countries buying the Starfighter in November 1960 when Lockheed granted another manufacturing license to a consortium of Italian firms headed by Fiat and including Aerfer-Macchi, Piaggio, SACA and SIAI-Marchetti. Eventually there were over 45 contractors and subcontractors involved in Starfighter production, and a NATO Starfighter Management Organization was established at Koblenz in the Federal Republic of Germany.

It was ironic that the sleek Starfighter, which had been designed as an air superiority fighter, was now being designated to serve as a *multirole aircraft*, which meant that it would have to serve as a fighter-bomber as well as an interceptor. The trim fighter designed with tiny wings for fast climbs to high altitudes was now being used as a bomb truck!

The first F-104G was flown in October 1960 at Lockheed's Palmdale, California factory and was followed by 30 Lockheed-built TF-104F two-seat trainers that were delivered to the Luftwaffe Training Command at Luke AFB, Arizona, where German Starfighter pilots were trained. The Canadian Starfighter first flew in May 1961, followed by the first German-built F-104G in August 1961. In 1962, the Luftwaffe's JBG-31 at Norvenich was the first wing in Germany to become operational with the F-104G, and by 1968 the German air arm was fully operational with the Starfighter. So, too, were those of Belgium, Canada, Italy, the Netherlands *and* Norway.

During the mid-1960s the F-104G developed a serious reputation for being accident-prone, and in fact, 1965 was witness to a Starfighter crash *every ten days*. As maintenance and pilot proficiency improved, however, the F-104G became a good deal more reliable.

In the late 1960s Lockheed and Fiat developed, and Fiat produced, an upgraded Starfighter designated F-104S because it was designed to carry the Sparrow air-to-air missile. The F-104S went on to serve with the air forces of both Greece and Turkey.

Aside from the various Starfighters used by the US Air Force and the CF-104 (basically an F-104F) built for Canada, the F-104G and F-104S have served—and continue to serve into the 1980s—with eight NATO air forces: Belgium, Denmark, Germany, Greece, Italy, the Netherlands, Norway and Turkey. Spain also used the Starfighter, but that was prior to its joining NATO.

Three major international cooperative efforts undertaken by NATO members in Europe which were not specifically done

The Panavia Tornado (*below right*) was custom designed as a multirole combat aircraft, to serve the long-term defense requirements of its builder—'Panavia'—a consortium of aircraft manufacturers in Germany, Great Britain and Italy. The fast, versatile and reliable Tornado is the centerpiece of the airforces of the Panavia partner nations.

under NATO auspices have been the SEPECAT Jaguar, the Dassault-Breguet/Dornier Alpha Jet and the Panavia Tornado.

The Jaguar is a supersonic attack aircraft developed jointly by British Aerospace and Breguet in France. It first flew in 1968 and entered service in 1972. Although the Jaguar has been exported to Ecuador, India and Oman, it is used only by Britain and France in Europe.

The diminutive Alpha Jet was designed to serve as a trainer as well as a light attack and reconnaissance aircraft. Built by Dassault-Breguet in France and Dornier in Germany, it first flew in 1973 and began to enter service with the air forces of France, Germany and Belgium in 1978.

The Panavia Tornado, discussed at length in photo captions throughout this text, is the most important combat aircraft project undertaken in Western Europe since World War II. It was developed by Panavia, a consortium formed in 1969 by Aeritalia in Italy, British Aerospace, and Messerschmitt-Bolkow-Blohm in Germany. Originally identified as a Multirole Combat Aircraft (MRCA), the Tornado faced the difficult and complex task of replacing everything from Mach 2 interceptors to strategic bombers. In effect, it was being designed *from the ground up* to do what the F-104G was *adapted* to do.

The Tornado prototype first flew in 1974, but it was not until 1980 that operational training began at the Tri-national Tornado Training Establishment (TTTE) at the RAF base at Cottesmore. Pilots from the air forces of the three Panavia partner nations, as well as Germany's Bundesmarine (Navy), learn to fly the Tornado at Cottesmore before being rotated to operational squadrons at home.

As a Multirole Combat Aircraft, the Tornado was designed for a variety of tactical combat duties. These center around air-superiority and the Interdictor Strike (IDS) or fighter-

bomber roles, but also include tactical reconnaissance. A specialized Tornado, the Air Defense Variant (ADV), has been ordered by Britain's RAF for use as an interceptor. The need for the Tornado ADV, or Tornado F-2 as it is called in service, becomes clear when one considers the vastness of the UK Air Defense Region, which stretches from Iceland to the English Channel and from the British Isles east to Norway.

Because of its speed, armament capacity and reliability, the Tornado is now an essential part of NATO's airpower from the Arctic to the Mediterranean.

NATO AIRPOWER'S CRUCIAL ROLE

It is axiomatic that air superiority over a modern battlefield is essential to winning any conflict, but for NATO the need is critical. Because NATO is outnumbered by the Warsaw Pact's conventional ground, as well as air, forces, the qualitative advantage that NATO enjoys in its aircraft might be the sole factor that would give NATO forces the edge in a potential confrontation, and in the meanwhile help to deter Warsaw Pact adventurism.

CHAPTER 2
An Introduction To The NATO Alliance
Prepared by the NATO Information Service

The North Atlantic Treaty Organization is a defensive alliance of sovereign and independent nations, founded on the principles of individual liberty and the rule of law. The Alliance aims to prevent war; indeed the ultimate political purpose of the Alliance is to achieve a lasting peaceful order accompanied by appropriate security guarantees. It works to achieve this by striving to improve understanding between East and West and by possessing sufficient strength to deter an attack on any member of the Alliance. The Treaty provides that Alliance members will come to each other's assistance in the event of an armed attack upon any one of them.

At the meeting of the North Atlantic Council at Bonn in June 1982, the Heads of State and Government declared: 'Our purpose is to prevent war, and while safeguarding democracy, to build the foundations of lasting peace. None of our weapons will ever be used except in response to attack. We respect the sovereignty, equality, independence and territorial integrity of all states. In fulfillment of our purpose, we shall maintain adequate military strength and political solidarity. On that basis, we will persevere in efforts to establish, whenever Soviet behavior makes this possible, a more constructive East-West relationship through dialogue, negotiation and mutually advantageous cooperation.'

While NATO must ensure that its defenses are adequate to meet any threat, it has consistently striven, through the pursuit of balanced, verifiable and militarily significant arms control agreements, to ensure security at a reduced level of armaments. The NATO governments continue to actively pursue reductions and limitations on conventional forces in Central Europe in the Mutual and Balanced Force Reductions (MBFR) talks in Vienna. At the Conference on Disarmament in Geneva, the United States has presented a comprehensive proposal for a complete ban on chemical weapons.

The size and type of forces which could be used against NATO influence the kinds of forces the Alliance needs to deter a military threat and thereby to prevent aggression in any

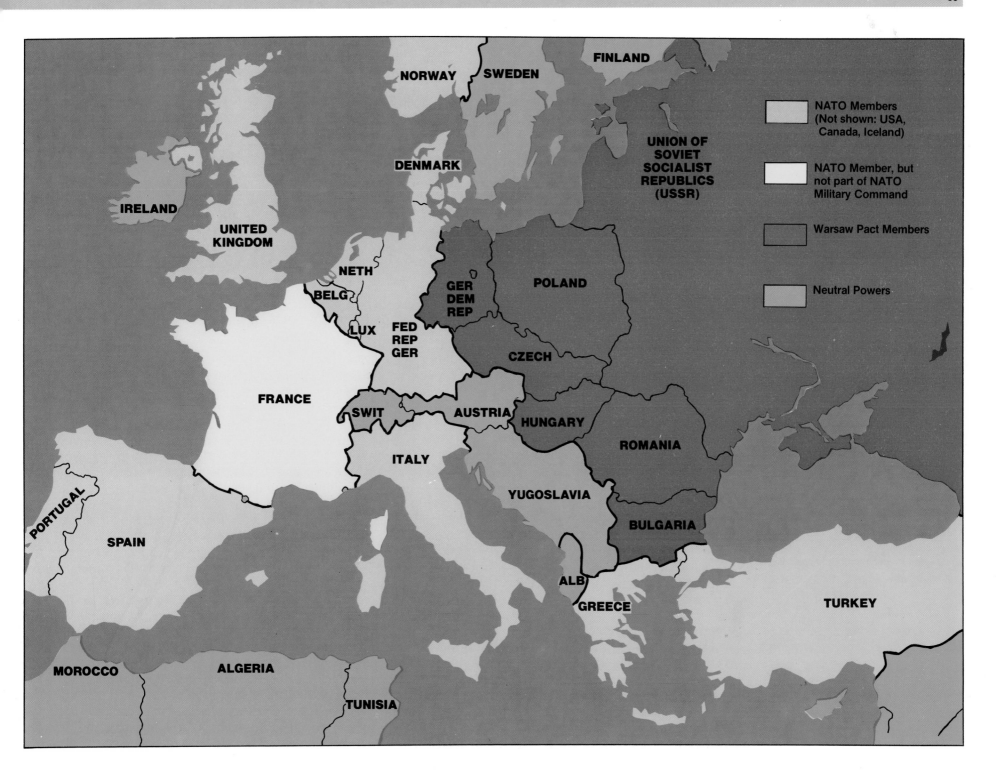

NORWAY SWEDEN FINLAND

IRELAND

UNITED KINGDOM

DENMARK

UNION OF SOVIET SOCIALIST REPUBLICS (USSR)

NETH

BELG

GER DEM REP

POLAND

LUX

FED REP GER

CZECH

FRANCE

SWIT

AUSTRIA

HUNGARY

ITALY

YUGOSLAVIA

ROMANIA

PORTUGAL

SPAIN

BULGARIA

ALB

GREECE

TURKEY

MOROCCO ALGERIA

TUNISIA

NATO Members (Not shown: USA, Canada, Iceland)

NATO Member, but not part of NATO Military Command

Warsaw Pact Members

Neutral Powers

US Strategic Air Power: *At the immediate right* is a view 'down the pavement' of a B-52G bomber packing a brace of cruise missile pods under its wings. The Air Launched Cruise Missiles (ALCMs) are released in quantity by the bomber, and fly low to the ground, using their Terrain-Avoidance Radar.

This ALCM launch capability greatly enhances the bomber's effectiveness, as the missiles can be programmed for targets up to a thousand miles apart—the B-52 thus 'strikes' against a very wide area, and considering the ALCM's nuclear punch, one B-52G so equipped could pose a tremendous deterrent threat anywhere in the European theater of operations.

On the opposite page, ground crew members install a pod of six ALCMs (arranged three up front-three behind on the pod) under the wing of a B-52G.

form. NATO as a defensive alliance does not seek superiority nor does it attempt to match the Warsaw Pact man for man or system for system. However, if peace and stability are to be preserved, the relationship between the overall military capabilities, both nuclear and conventional, of NATO and the Warsaw Pact must not become so unbalanced that the credibility of NATO's deterrent could be called into question. In other words, the Alliance requires enough forces of the right kinds to make it clear that it would be able to respond to any type of aggression in an effective way. The NATO deterrent comprises conventional forces, intermediate- and short-range nuclear forces and strategic nuclear forces. Adequate conventional forces are required in order to deprive the Warsaw Pact of the chance of military success without recourse to other capabilities. To achieve this, NATO's conventional forces must be capable of the forward defense of NATO's territories and the safeguarding of the sea lines of communication.

The United States strategic nuclear forces are the ultimate guarantee of NATO's security in that they link an aggressor's decision to attack with the incalculable risk of total destruction. Well balanced intermediate- and short-range nuclear forces are essential to NATO as the link between the conventional and strategic legs of the NATO Triad. Possession of

these capabilities is necessary to enable the Alliance to choose amongst a number of options and to ensure that an aggressor is left in no doubt about NATO's readiness and will to defend itself while leaving it uncertain about the form that defense would take. This is the essence of NATO's overall strategy known as 'flexible response.' For deterrence to be effective the Alliance must be able both to make credible its capability and willingness to defend itself and to make the risks unacceptable for any potential aggressor.

The Warsaw Pact leadership has repeatedly stated that its organization is also strictly defensive in nature. However, past and present policies have contradicted their statements. The Warsaw Pact's military strength is on a scale well in excess of that reasonably justifiable for defense. The Warsaw Pact maintains large-scale strategic nuclear forces, intermediate- and short-range nuclear forces and massive conventional forces. Moreover, Warsaw Pact military strategy, as shown by its literature and military exercises, calls for large-scale penetration into enemy territory in order to secure strategic objectives; it continues to emphasize the element of surprise and the necessity of rapid offensive operations.

Warsaw Pact forces are organized and equipped and trained to take the offensive right from the beginning of a conflict. This involves combined arms operations in which all forces,

A Luftwaffe Panavia Tornado IDS (*below*) does a banking turn over European forests and 'cowpatch' countryside. The Tornado's wing lift coefficient is probably the highest of any supersonic aircraft, and despite being designed to tote a wider variety of ordnance than any other tactical aircraft in history, at sea level in clean condition the Tornado IDS is currently the fastest combat aircraft ever built. *Is gutt!*

Opposite page: An Iceland-based USAF Tactical Air Command F-15 Eagle intercepts a mean ol' Soviet Air Force DA (Long Range Aviation) squadron Tu-20 (aka Tu-95) Bear long-range strategic bomber. The F-15 is the *creme de la creme* of the USAF fighters, and the veriest hot rod of the 'Eagle Drivers'— F-15 pilots.

The Bear Bomber progressed from the Tupolev Tu-4 Bull, which was a direct rip-off of B-29 design. Though its swept-wing design defies all common sense for a propeller plane, the Bear's huge turbo-props can drag it along at 540 mph on un-refueled voyages of up to 11,000 miles.

conventional and nuclear, can be brought to bear in a unified manner, using all necessary assets. To this end, some fundamental reorganization and restructuring of Soviet forces has been in progress for several years and is still incomplete. The main outcome has been leaner combat units with proportionately higher combat power in support of updated tactics and concepts. For example, the reorganization of the Soviet tank and motorized divisions results in an increased number of tanks and especially artillery pieces. With regard to the air forces, the control of the Soviet Strategic and Tactical Bomber forces has been centralized recently under the command of four air armies in those parts of the Warsaw Pact which face NATO. Soviet military capabilities would enable the use of chemical weapons on a large scale.

COMPARING NATO AND WARSAW PACT FORCES

Many factors contribute to the capability to deter or defend against aggression. These include political and social stability, geography, economic strength, human resources, industrial and technological resources, as well as military capabilities. The military forces possessed by each side are clearly important but are not the only elements in this equation, and in comparing each side's military forces it is important to avoid over-simplification. A complete assessment of the global balance of power would have to take into account forces other than those that are available to NATO and the Warsaw Pact. Even if consideration was to be restricted to NATO and the Warsaw Pact capabilities only, a full assessment would have to

take into account not just the conventional forces deployed by each side in Europe but also certain worldwide deployments by a number of NATO countries as well as by the Soviet Union. For instance, both the United States and the Soviet Union maintain substantial forces in Asia and the Pacific.

In addition to quantifiable force differences there are also other elements important to an understanding of the balance. These include, for example, differences in military strategy and structure, political organization and cohesion, the qualitative aspect of forces and the availability of timely reinforcements. Other important considerations are the amount of ammunition, fuel and other stocks possessed by each side, the quality of their equipment, the quality of their civil and military infrastructure, their organization, their personnel, their leadership and morale, as well as each side's economic, industrial and technological ability to sustain a military conflict.

Geographic and economic dissimilarities between NATO and the Warsaw Pact directly affect the roles and missions of their armed forces. For example, the Warsaw Pact is one geographic entity in contrast to NATO, which is separated by oceans, seas and in some regions, particularly in the south, by the territory of nations which are not members of the Alliance. This allows the Warsaw Pact to transfer land and air forces and support between different areas via internal and generally secure lines of communication. It also contributes to enabling the Warsaw Pact to select the time and place in which to concentrate its forces. However, Soviet naval forces are divided into four widely separated fleets; this makes it difficult for them to mass naval power for joint operations or to maintain an effective naval presence for sustained periods away from home ports.

NATO, on the other hand, must transfer resources along lengthy and vulnerable air and sea routes to and around Europe. The most powerful partner in NATO, the United States, is separated from its European allies by an ocean 3700 miles wide. Moreover, NATO nations, to a far greater extent than those of the Warsaw Pact, depend on shipping for vital economic purposes. Thus, unlike the Warsaw Pact, NATO has a fundamental dependence on shipping during peace and war. This fact requires markedly different missions for Warsaw Pact naval forces on the one hand and NATO naval forces on the other. Additionally, NATO lacks geographical depth in Europe between the possible areas of conflict and the coasts, thus rendering its rear areas, headquarters and supplies more vulnerable to enemy attack and more difficult to defend.

Opposite page: A Soviet ground crew tightens up the engines of a Tupolev Tu-22 'Blinder' supersonic bomber. This particular plane is outfitted as a basic reconnaissance craft — the Tu-22's effectiveness as a supersonic high penetration bomber was much reduced by the development of Western Mach 2 interceptors such as the Panavia Tornado and the McDonnell Douglas F-15 Eagle, to name two.

Below: A USAFE F-4E 'tub' (two-seater) intercepts a Tu-95 Bear. Not a hot situation, just two planes in neutral airspace, a little too close to NATO territory. Just in case, though, the thing under the F-4's chin is a 20mm cannon, and aft of that is a pair of AIM-7 Sparrow air-to-air missiles.

The Warsaw Pact nations have a standing force of some six million personnel of which some four million face NATO in Europe. In addition, there are over 800,000 personnel with some military training enrolled in the national security forces. Warsaw Pact active and reserve forces worldwide include 246 divisions plus 29 brigades, with 61,000 main battle tanks and air forces equipped with nearly 13,000 aircraft. Ground and air forces in Europe are forward deployed, well structured, positioned and prepared for offensive operations. The Warsaw Pact possesses an impressive inventory of naval forces, the largest component of which is the Soviet Navy. In addition to ballistic missile submarines Warsaw Pact active naval forces include nearly 290 other submarines (a number of which are equipped to launch Cruise missiles), about 40 major surface combatant ships (*Kiev* class ships and cruisers) and about 400 naval bombers (most of which are equipped to deliver anti-ship missiles). A large number of these forces are not in the NATO/Warsaw Pact area and indeed some, primarily those of the Soviet Union, are deployed worldwide. Overall, the War-

Opposite page and above: The Soviet MiG-23 'Flogger' swing-wing fighter can do Mach 2.31, and is set up for a variety of armament. The standard fighter of the Soviet air force, the MiG-23 is the most numerous aircraft in service with any air force in the world. Export variants, with reduced avionic standard, smaller radar, and similar reductions have been farmed out to various Soviet satellites and 'friendly' nations, especially in Eastern Europe and in the Middle East. Given the Soviets' continuing adjustments and improvements to its basic design, the MiG-23 will probably be 'a contender' for years to come.

Bitburg-based USAFE F-15 Eagles (*above*) symbolically canopy a bit of Central European tradition. NATO bases receive steady resupply from the US via such air transports as the enormous USAF Lockheed C-5B Galaxy (*above right*) and the very versatile Lockheed C-130 Hercules (*opposite*).

saw Pact has, in recent years, significantly improved the quality of equipment in all components of its armed forces: strategic, ground, air and naval.

The standing forces of the NATO nations total 4.5 million personnel, of which nearly 2.6 million are stationed in Europe. There are also nearly 400,000 other militarily trained personnel, such as Home Guards and Gendarmerie. Total active and reserve forces belonging to NATO nations, but not all committed to NATO, include 82 divisions and over 180 independent brigades (normally in NATO three brigades equal one division), with about 25,000 main battle tanks and air forces equipped with approximately 11,200 combat aircraft. NATO forces are well trained and, given the full range of capabilities at their disposal, are capable of presenting a credible defense of Alliance territory. In most NATO countries, modern and effective aircraft, tanks and anti-tank weapons are being introduced into the armed forces.

THE PROBLEMS OF MOBILIZATION AND REINFORCEMENT

NATO and Warsaw Pact forces rely heavily on the mobilization of reservists to bring active duty formations up to strength and to man mobilizable formations. However, the closely controlled social structures of the Warsaw Pact nations and the length and intensiveness of the training of their military conscripts permit them to maintain a more significant pool of trained reserve manpower than is maintained by NATO.

The bulk of NATO's reinforcements of men and equipment must be moved across the Atlantic and the English Channel largely by sea. The Warsaw Pact, on the other hand, can move many of its central reserves rapidly by means of internal road, rail and air links. NATO could not sustain an effective defense against these reinforced Warsaw Pact forces solely with in-place forces. Therefore a successful defense would be largely dependent upon the timely arrival of substantial reinforcements, principally from the United States, but also from Canada and in Europe itself from the United Kingdom and Portugal. However, the problems would be considerable even with reasonable warning time. The rapid reinforcement of land forces is a very complex operation that demands the timely availability of numerous resources, particularly transport aircraft and shipping as well as reception and prepositioned equipment storage facilities. Reinforcement of air forces involves infrastructure and logistic problems of a different but also complex nature, particularly in the areas of sur-

German paratroopers of the Allied Command Europe receive instructions from an officer (*above*). *At right:* ACE forces gather at a West German airfield. The large prop plane at the far right is a Luftwaffe Transall C-160D troop and cargo transport. Note the RAF truck in the foreground.

vivability and combat support. While there are a considerable number of reinforcement air squadrons available to cross the Atlantic within a few hours, they could have to wait for the subsequent arrival of their ground crew and support equipment before they could become operational.

LAND FORCES

Warsaw Pact forces facing Allied Command Europe (ACE), which is the NATO military command which stretches from the northern tip of Norway to the eastern borders of Turkey, consist of about 167 active and mobilizable divisions plus the equivalent of nine divisions of airborne, air assault and airmobile formations, which could be used in a number of different areas. Taking account of the forces of the non-Soviet Warsaw Pact countries, the Soviet forces located in those countries, but only the high readiness forces of the six Western Military Districts of the Soviet Union, there are some 115 divisions positioned well forward or considered ready to fight

Opposite page: A West German border patrol leader (holding cup) and his men cast wary glances across the line as East German troops engage in tactical exercises (in the background).

The comparatively small Warsaw Pact ground divisions supplement their low manpower with armor and artillery. The two Soviet T-64A main battle tanks *at left* were photographed on maneuvers in Eastern Europe.

The T-64 tank is the mainstay of Warsaw Pact armored strength—it has replaced the T-55 main battle tank by dint of its rapid-fire (eight rounds per minute) cannon and other improvements.

Another Warsaw Pact armor infantry backup is the BTR-50P amphibian (shown *below* unloading Soviet naval infantry), which standard armament consists of one 12.7mm and one to three 7.62mm machine guns.

at very short notice. Moreover, these standing Warsaw Pact forces can be reinforced by about 16 divisions from the Strategic Reserve based in the central Military Districts of Russia (Moscow, Ural and Volga Military Districts).

Warsaw Pact divisions normally consist of fewer personnel than NATO divisions but contain more tanks and artillery, thereby producing similar combat power. Their principal offensive conventional capabilities consist of tanks, modern mechanized infantry vehicles and highly mobile long-range artillery and mortars; large numbers of these are to be found in all their units. Soviet forces posses a wide variety of chemical agents and delivery systems and are the best equipped in the world to sustain operations in a chemical environment. Growing numbers of transport, support and attack helicopters provide the Warsaw Pact with a quick assault and reaction capability, and with a supplement to their fixed-wing tactical aircraft in the battlefield area.

Land forces committed to NATO and stationed in or rapidly deployable to Europe, consist of the equivalent of some 88 active and mobilizable divisions (including three airborne/air mobile divisions), many of which are also ready to fight at very short notice. There are, in addition, the equivalent of 12

active United States divisions plus one Armored Cavalry regiment, two United States Marine divisions and a Canadian brigade in North America which could be made available in Europe in due course. Four of these United States divisions have their equipment prepositioned in Europe. Almost half of NATO's tank and mechanized divisions are equipped with modern weapons, although a very unfavorable ratio continues between NATO anti-tank guided weapons and Warsaw Pact tanks and armored personnel vehicles. NATO similarly has a lower proportion of armed attack helicopters. Only the United States has a retaliatory chemical capability, and a number of NATO nations lack even adequate protection against chemical weapons.

AIR FORCES AND AIR DEFENSE FORCES

The overall global total of Warsaw Pact aircraft is nearly 13,000.* More than 10,000* of these are facing NATO Europe, of which 7500* are of types technically capable of delivering nuclear weapons. The majority of these aircraft would likely be used in conventional attacks over NATO Europe. The total number of combat aircraft in operational units facing NATO Europe is over 7000. Warsaw Pact air defense forces as far east as the Urals (but excluding those in the Moscow Military and Air Defense Districts) consist of some 4000 interceptor/air-combat aircraft. Many of these aircraft can be used in offensive roles such as assuring air superiority over the battlefield, and they are backed up by extensive modern surface-to-air missile systems. Additionally there are some 2250 ground-attack fighter bombers, 585 reconnaissance aircraft and about 400 bombers (including 65 Backfire bombers), the majority of which would likely be used in a conventional role.

The Backfire and other strategic bombers, however, are dealt with in the nuclear section. These air forces could be reinforced rapidly with some 540 combat aircraft from central Russia. Significant numbers of new combat aircraft are introduced each year, replacing older models which were less capable than NATO aircraft of the same generation. The introduction of these modern tactical aircraft has considerably increased the Warsaw Pact's offensive capability. These latest

*These totals include all aircraft of combat types including those in non-combat units as well as combat units (a criterion essential for arms control); all other numbers are based on aircraft in combat units.

aircraft are capable of carrying up to twice the payload, can travel over three times the range, at higher speeds, and can conduct operations at lower altitudes than the aircraft they are replacing; this renders them less vulnerable to NATO air defenses. Their increased combat radius would allow for Warsaw Pact operations from more distant bases in case of Warsaw Pact aggression against NATO. This would mean that NATO fighter-bombers would have to penetrate much deeper into defended enemy airspace to counter-attack Warsaw Pact airbases. Additionally, an increasing proportion of these modern aircraft can operate in adverse weather conditions by day or by night.

The Warsaw Pact airlift capability is substantial. Soviet military transport aviation alone, consisting of over 600 long-and medium-range aircraft, provides sufficient airlift to transport one complete airborne division and its equipment at any one

Above: An eager *praporshchik* (Soviet warrant officer) reads *Malaya Zemlya* (*The Far Lands*), which is one of the three volumes of the late President Leonid Brezhnev's autobiography. While military officers are not particular favorites in Soviet society at large, they enjoy many special privileges as Party members in good standing.

Opposite: The Soviet Tu-26 Backfire medium-range nuclear bomber and strike aircraft can carry 17,500 lbs of stores, including the AS-4 Kitchen air-to-surface missile or the AS-6 Kingfish anti-shipping missile; has a combat radius of over 3000 miles and a sustained 'dash' speed of 1180 mph; and is loaded with targeting electronics.

Above: A Royal Norwegian Air Force P-3 Orion anti-submarine warfare aircraft cruises the cliffs of a snowclad fjord. The Lockheed P-3 Orion does reconnaissance, surveillance and combat duty for many NATO members, and for many other countries throughout the world.

Northern Region airpower—A Norwegian AF F-104G Super Starfighter (*opposite page*) knifes the air above Norway's very rugged countryside, which is a great defense against ground attack, since the tough terrain makes land movement difficult, if not impossible. Note the arresting hook under the aft section of this bird, which is symbolic of the country's dearth of smooth, flat earth for long runways.

time up to distances of 1200 miles. This capability can be supplemented in particular by Aeroflot civilian aircraft.

The overall global total of aircraft belonging to NATO countries is slightly more than 11,000. The land-based air forces, available in-place for NATO's Allied Command Europe, consist of roughly 2000 ground-attack fighter bombers, 800 interceptors and 250 reconnaissance aircraft. In addition to fighting the air battle, air forces would have to assist NATO ground forces in repulsing a Warsaw Pact attack. The United States and Canada could reinforce rapidly with over 1700 more combat aircraft, though airlift would be required for ground crews and equipment. The quality of NATO aircraft has improved with the introduction into service of the F-15, F-16 and the Tornado. These aircraft have a greater range, payload and all-weather capability than the previous generation of NATO aircraft. However, since NATO and Warsaw Pact aircraft now have comparable range and payload characteristics, the quantitative advantage of the Warsaw Pact is more significant than formerly.

NATO's military airlift assets consist of nearly 750 transport aircraft, which can be augmented by the civil air fleets of the Allied countries. These are considerably larger than the civil air fleets available to the Warsaw Pact. However, the latter are centrally controlled.

NATO nations have made considerable progress in improving the ability of their air forces to operate and survive in a hostile environment, particularly by providing better protection for vital operational and logistical facilities. To a considerable degree, NATO air forces maintain a high state of readiness and are qualitatively superior to those of the Warsaw Pact in terms of training and weapons systems. The tactical flexibility of NATO air forces and the ability to augment in-place forces rapidly in time of tension or war are also positive factors.

Warsaw Pact forces have an extensive range of static and mobile air defenses, including a variety of surface-to-air missiles and guns.

MARITIME FORCES

As noted earlier, there are fundamental differences in the missions of the naval forces of the Warsaw Pact and NATO that result from geographic and economic dissimilarities. The security of NATO nations depends on the unimpeded use of the sea both to link the potential of North America and Europe and to provide access for trade, raw materials and energy. The role of the NATO navies, as for all NATO forces, is in the first instance to deter aggression. They must be able to demonstrate a capability in peace and take action in war to preserve, protect and maintain the sea lines of communication, neutralize hostile forces, and to project maritime power in support of land and air forces.

In other words, the role of NATO maritime forces is sea control, which means using the seas for NATO's purposes. Conversely, as continental powers, the Warsaw Pact nations have far less dependence on the sea. The role of their navies includes the denial to NATO of its use of maritime power, the disruption of NATO's sea lines of communication and possibly the conduct and support of amphibious operations in North Norway, on the Baltic exits and in Northern Turkey.

The Warsaw Pact navies include an increasingly modernized submarine force which poses a serious threat to NATO's sea lines of communication. There is also a wide range of modern surface vessels fitted with anti-submarine weapons systems, anti-air missiles and some which carry fixed-wing aircraft and/or helicopters. The capabilities of these naval forces, complemented by a force of land-based naval attack aircraft, include stand-off weapons and cruise missiles.

NORTHERN AND CENTRAL REGION LAND FORCES

Warsaw Pact forces facing this area consist of the equivalent of some 104 divisions drawn from the armies of the Soviet Union, German Democratic Republic, Czechoslovakia and Poland and deploying some 28,000 tanks and 20,000 artillery and mortar pieces. In the far north the Warsaw Pact has two Soviet divisions. Farther south within the same Military District are an additional seven divisions including one airborne division. The equivalent of 95 divisions face the southern part of the Northern Region and Central Europe. Of these, the equivalent of almost 61 divisions with 17,000 tanks and 10,000 artillery and mortar pieces are either deployed in the forward areas or are held at high states of readiness. The Warsaw Pact also has considerable amphibious capabilities in the Barents Sea and the Baltic.

Opposing the Warsaw Pact, NATO's in-place and rapidly deployable land forces are composed of armed forces from Belgium, Canada, Denmark, the Federal Republic of Germany, Luxembourg, the Netherlands, Norway, the United

Kingdom and the United States. The in-place and rapidly deployable land forces of NATO in this area consist of the equivalent of nearly 43 divisions including those forces in the United Kingdom, fielding about 8165 tanks and 4920 artillery and mortar pieces including prepositioned equipment. Most of these Northern and Central Region land forces are kept in a high state of readiness, but deficiencies include some maldeployment, and lines of supply which run too near and parallel to the border.

All NATO formations are dependent in varying degrees on mobilization and redeployment; despite these problems approximately 75 percent of these forces could be in position very quickly indeed. There are in addition active and mobilizable United States forces located in North America amounting to some 20 divisions and 24 brigades which, together with their associated equipment and tanks, drawn from an overall total of some 4100 tanks and 3670 artillery/mortars, could be available to move to Europe in due course. Some of these could be allocated to the Southern Region. Up to three of the divisions would arrive quickly by air. Other United States divisions, with their equipment, would arrive later by sea. A Canadian brigade group would also reinforce the area.

Some 61 of the 104 divisions in the German Democratic Republic, Czechoslovakia, Poland and the Northern and Western Military Districts of the Soviet Union could launch operations within a few days of mobilization. In the best situation, assuming simultaneous mobilization and deployment forward within the region, NATO could count on the equivalent of nearly 43 divisions, which would have to hold out until additional United States and Canadian forces arrive by sea. In the meantime, the Warsaw Pact forces could be quickly expanded to their full 104 divisions, plus a proportion of the 16 Strategic Reserve Divisions from the three Central Military Districts.

NORTHERN AND CENTRAL REGION AIR FORCES

The Warsaw Pact is numerically superior in terms of fixed-wing tactical aircraft in this area. The NATO figures shown below include United Kingdom based aircraft and United States aircraft based in Europe in peacetime. The high proportion of ground-attack fighter bomber aircraft in NATO air forces is partly required to counter the Warsaw Pact preponderance in armor on the Central Front. Against this force, however, the Warsaw Pact can deploy interceptor forces,

many of which can also be used for ground attack, and exceptionally strong surface-to-air defense systems. Aircraft of the Moscow Military and Air Defense District are excluded from the following table because of their distance from the Northern and Southern Regions. Also nearly 1800 United States and Canadian-based reinforcement aircraft, which are situated even further from these regions, are excluded.

NORTHERN AND CENTRAL REGIONS IN-PLACE AIR FORCES

	Fighter-Bomber Ground-Attack	Interceptors	Reconnaissance
NATO	1345	500	145
WARSAW PACT	1555	2635	390

(NB Some interceptors can be used in ground attack roles.)

SOUTHERN REGION LAND FORCES

The Warsaw Pact has 10 Soviet and Hungarian divisions, equipped with over 2340 tanks and 1560 artillery pieces which could be employed against Northeast Italy. These divisions, located in Hungary, could be reinforced by seven more divisions including 2000 tanks and 1300 artillery pieces coming from the Kiev Military District. These seven divisions, however, are not maintained at high states of readiness. Warsaw Pact forces additionally include the equivalent of three divisions of airborne, air mobile and air assault troops which could be used anywhere within the region. Furthermore, options against the Central Mediterranean could be possible. NATO land forces consist of the equivalent of eight Italian divisions (ie, four divisions and 12 independent brigades) with 1250 tanks and 1400 artillery and mortar pieces. The Italian forces are generally well deployed and improvements are planned to meet the support requirements for their reinforcement. Portugal also participates in the collective defense of this region by providing a reinforcement brigade for deployment in Northern Italy.

Replacements for the F-104: NATO F-16s from (*opposite, top down*) Norway; Denmark; Belgium; USAFE based at Hahn, West Germany; and the Netherlands—ride herd on a pocket of air above Belgium. Note the powder burnt gun ports of the Norwegian and (less extensively so) Belgian planes.

Above: An American tank commander takes a vigilant break as US armored strength lines up for NATO exercises in the Federal Republic.

Above: Camouflaged Italian troops tighten up their equipment before boarding the US Air Force Military Airlift Command Hercules troop transport in the background.

Opposite: A Greek Air Force F-4 Phantom flies the dusty blue above Mediterranean landscape. Though a two-seater 'tub,' the hottest F-4 can do Mach 2.27 at the top of the line, and is built to tote 16,000 lbs of accessory armament—and that ain't *souvlaki.*

The equivalent of 34 Soviet, Romanian and Bulgarian divisions are available in the area north of Greece and Turkish Thrace. These forces are largely mechanized and are equipped with roughly 6600 tanks and over 6400 artillery and mortar pieces. They are on terrain suitable for armoured offensive operations and could be reinforced by amphibious forces and by the Warsaw Pact airborne/air mobile divisions referred to above. Of these 34 divisions, the equivalent of just over 22 divisions with 3680 tanks and 2940 artillery and mortar pieces are either deployed forward or are maintained at high states of readiness. NATO's 25 Greek and Turkish divisions in the area are mainly infantry. Their task is rendered difficult for defensive operations by the narrowness of the area between the borders and the Aegean.

Spain joined the NATO Alliance in 1982, but does not commit its forces to NATO's military commands, and is not fully integrated into the Alliance's military structure.

SOUTHERN REGION AIR FORCES

As with other regions, the flexibility of air forces renders comparison difficult. In-place forces available to the Warsaw Pact and NATO are approximately as follows:

SOUTHERN REGION/IN-PLACE AIR FORCES

	Fighter-Bomber Ground-Attack	Interceptors	Reconnaissance
NATO	615	295	90
WARSAW PACT	695	1560	195

(NB Some interceptors can be used in ground attack roles.)

The range of some of the modern Warsaw Pact aircraft is such that they have the potential to operate anywhere in the Mediterranean, endangering the security of sea lines of communication which are of vital importance to the NATO nations in the Southern Flank. The geography of the Mediterranean emphasizes the interaction between the maritime land and air situations. The NATO naval forces and Soviet Mediterranean

Above: A ground crew member makes sure that the pilot of this F-15 can see all around him, clearly. Despite the F-15's sophisticated sensing gear, there is no substitute for a good pair of fighter jock eyes.

The SAC equivalent of the USAFE F-111, this FB-111 Aardvark (*right*) is at heart the same solid airplane. Never a fighter, the 'Vark' is a dependable and versatile attack bomber, with nuclear capability. The FB-111 shown here wears six M-117 750-pound general purpose bombs under each wing.

Now you see them. . . The advantages of the mobile launching system concept are apparent in this photo (*opposite*) of a Ground Launched Cruise Missile (GLCM) launcher—aka Transporter Erector Launcher—a handy item in the world of NATO IRBMs.

Squadron would have to face opposing land-based and naval aviation; naval operations would in turn greatly influence land/air operations in the three sub-regions. External air reinforcements from the Alliance could be of crucial importance.

NUCLEAR DETERRENCE AND THE NUCLEAR EQUATION

As part of NATO's strategy, nuclear forces exist in combination with conventional forces to maintain peace through deterring aggression. To deter successfully, NATO's nuclear forces must be viewed by the Warsaw Pact as being credible by providing a wide range of options for their use in response to aggression. They must be, and be seen to be, capable of being employed effectively and adequately, to convince a potential aggressor that in any attack against NATO the costs would outweigh any conceivable gains.

At the same time, it is NATO's policy to maintain these forces at the lowest level capable of deterring the Warsaw Pact threat, taking account of developments in conventional as well as nuclear forces. In pursuance of this policy, NATO decided in October 1983 at Montebello, Canada to reduce the number of warheads in Europe by 1400 over the following five to six years, in addition to the withdrawal of 1000 warheads com-

pleted in 1980 independently of any arms control agreement. Moreover, this overall reduction of 2400 warheads in NATO's stockpile in Europe will not be affected by the deployment of Longer-Range INF (LRINF) missiles since one further warhead will be removed for each PERSHING II or Ground-Launched Cruise Missile (GLCM) warhead deployed, as envisaged in the December 1979 dual-track decision. This sustained program of reductions will reduce NATO's nuclear stockpile in Europe to the lowest level in over 20 years.

INTERMEDIATE-RANGE NUCLEAR FORCE AIRCRAFT

The ranges of aircraft vary considerably depending on the height and speed at which they are flown and how much they are carrying. Normally, the majority of INF aircraft carry only one warhead, but some types, particularly those with longer ranges, can carry two or three. Their coverage could also depend on the location of suitably equipped bases through which aircraft could transit or to which they could return. The comparisons that follow in this section cover land-based aircraft located in NATO Europe and, in the case of the Warsaw Pact, opposite NATO Europe. The Backfire bomber with its primary nuclear role has been included in the strategic section be-

cause it has an inherent intercontinental capability. However, in its maritime and European land-attack roles the Backfire also poses a serious nuclear and conventional threat to NATO Europe.

The comparison of longer-range INF aircraft in operational units shows that the Warsaw Pact has a considerable numerical advantage. NATO has about 150 F-111 aircraft in Europe; the Soviet Union has about 325 nuclear-capable Badgers and Blinders in its Strategic Aviation forces and an additional 175 aircraft of these types in the Soviet Naval Aviation (SNA) forces, making a total of 500 longer-range INF aircraft. This total excludes BADGERs and BLINDERs not configured for weapons delivery, such as those for Electronic Counter Measures (ECM), reconnaissance and air-to-air refuelling. It also excludes trainers that can be used on combat missions. Both the United States and the Soviet Union maintain longer-range INF aircraft outside Europe (in the United States and in the Soviet Far East, respectively).

Most of the types of combat aircraft of both NATO and the Warsaw Pact are technically capable of delivering nuclear weapons, but not all of these aircraft would be available for nuclear use for a variety of reasons. A substantial portion of these aircraft would be assigned to conventional missions, and

not all pilots who fly these aircraft are trained to deliver nuclear weapons. Taking these factors into account, it is estimated that overall the Warsaw Pact could employ about 3000 of its operational INF aircraft in a nuclear role. On the NATO side, the number of operational aircraft committed to a nuclear role is about 700. For NATO, decreases since 1982 in the area of INF aircraft are mainly due to the retirement of United Kingdom Vulcan bombers and the ongoing replacement of older aircraft with F-16 and Tornado. For the Warsaw Pact, the number of INF aircraft has increased through the further deployment of Flogger and Fencer aircraft. Thereby, the Warsaw Pact has increased even further its numerical advantage over NATO with regard to INF aircraft.

MILITARY PRODUCTION AND TECHNOLOGY CAPABILITIES

NATO and the Warsaw Pact each possess an extensive armaments production capability. In NATO, the capability is largely the aggregate output of a limited number of major arms producing nations, whose defense industries both compete and co-operate in producing equipment to meet NATO needs. There is thus no centralized procurement in NATO; indeed the sovereignty of NATO member countries is particularly evident in equipment procurement decisions, and all nations possess distinctive materiel acquisition systems and procurement regulations.

The situation in the Warsaw Pact could hardly be more different. One nation—the Soviet Union—dominates armaments production and exerts strong influence over the planning and procurement of the other Pact countries. The Soviet procurement process is based on rigorous, conservative planning with the result that risk taking is minimized. The consequence is a degree of inflexibility, but this discipline helps new equipment programs to keep to planning schedules. Nevertheless, subsequent upgrading of designs often occurs with modified variants of the original weapon systems appearing only a few years after the basic design.

These contrasting acquisition processes bring their own advantages and disadvantages. The processes of the NATO member nations are based on, and serve to encourage, an efficient, responsive defense industry that has to compete in the market place. In doing so, moreover, it draws heavily on the more advanced civilian technologies of the West to improve its products. The Soviet system, on the other hand, is extremely bureaucratic, and although it shows relatively fast development and deployment of weapons, it does not always facilitate the speediest translation of new technology into weapons design.

There is one area where the centralized acquisition process in the Warsaw Pact yields important dividends as compared to the decentralized processes in NATO—and that is standardization. Coalition warfare places an exacting premium on the ability of equipment of different forces to work together. The high degree of standardization in the Warsaw Pact is contrasted, on the NATO side, by glaring examples not only of a lack of interoperability, but of the danger of mutual interference.

In the area of production technology, the Soviet Union has developed the largest forging and extrusion presses in the world. It has considerable expertise in heavy manufacturing and engineering and, as a result, it has a lead over NATO nations in its ability to produce large, single piece components. However, NATO nations continue to lead in the area of automated manufacturing technology, such as numerically controlled machine tools and high precision equipment. Present trends indicate that the Warsaw Pact will continue to out-produce NATO in major military systems.

TECHNOLOGY

Technology is an important gauge of industrial and military strength. However, the differences in the levels of military technology between NATO and the Warsaw Pact cannot be usefully summarized in general terms since the picture varies from one technology or weapon system to another. Any discussion of technology differences is inevitably selective. Nevertheless, a comparison of trends shows that the Soviet Union, which is the undisputed technological leader of the Warsaw Pact, is making significant progress in areas where NATO has previously been leading. Moreover, when it considers it to be to its advantage, the Soviet Union does not hesitate to take advantage of the freedom of Western societies in order to acquire Western technology/equipment and know-how.

NATO nations until recently enjoyed clear leadership in most areas of technology, though, as noted above, this lead is being eroded. A major reason for this is that the level of resources devoted to military related research and development in NATO nations has not in general kept pace with worldwide inflationary trends, and the increasing costs involved in moving into new technology areas.

CHAPTER 3
NATO Strategy: Competition vs. Stability

From remarks delivered by

Under Secretary of Defense for Policy Fred Ikle

to the Wehrkunde conference, Munich, Germany, 2 March 1986.

Opposite: US troops take part in an exercise in West Germany, which was aimed at approximating their potential wartime environment. Using chartered buses was an expedient and a trial, of sorts, for variant modes of transportation.

Many of us remember, as a personal experience, the Second World War. It was this shared experience of wartime anguish and postwar hope that moved the people of Western Europe and North America to create our great Alliance. Over the years now, we all have become habituated to our Alliance. It seems to fit like an old shoe. Its institutions have become comfortable bureaucracies. The annual rhythm of its meetings and exercises has become reassuring, like some familiar liturgy. Today, all nations that cherish liberty have become dependent on our alliance, not only within NATO's formal boundaries, but the free nations outside as well—from Sweden to Australia, from Japan to Austria. The Atlantic Alliance is the global guardian of the democratic order: like Atlas, it is holding up our world.

The results of this quest for stability are, at best, a mixture of successes and failures. The territorial integrity of the Alliance, without question, has been fully preserved in peace. Contrast this accomplishment with the fate of the Korean peninsula, where the integrity of the Republic in the South was restored only by a costly war. But this unquestionable success in

Above: A Soviet MiG-23 (NATO code-named 'Flogger') being prepped for take-off.

Opposite: Note the large, maneuverability-enhancing outer wing slats affixed to this USAFE 17th Air Force F-4 Phantom II, which by its tail code and fin flash shows that it is based at Spangdahlem with the 336th TFS of the 4th TFW.

Europe doesn't mean that our Alliance is safely sheltered from the wars and instability in the rest of the world.

Furthermore, the efforts to stabilize the arms competition did not bring the hoped-for results. We embraced the idea in the 1960s that if both East and West agreed to leave themselves totally vulnerable to the other side's nuclear attack, neither would see a need or purpose for continuing to build up offensive nuclear arms. For many in the West, such a stable relationship of consensual, mutual vulnerability was the rationale that led us to the Anti-Ballistic Missile Treaty.

Some 20 years later, we now realize that the Soviet leaders held to different objectives. They had never settled for consensual vulnerability. Of course, they were quite ready to consent to the self-chosen vulnerability of the West. But for themselves they had other ideas. They built up their offensive forces, launched a huge construction effort for underground command posts to protect the Nomenklatura from nuclear war, and continued large programs to improve air and missile defenses.

Winston Churchill once remarked: 'However absorbed a commander may be in the elaboration of his own thoughts, it is necessary sometimes to take the enemy into consideration.'

Failure to take the enemy into consideration is a pervasive weakness of a democratic alliance. Many of us are hesitant even to admit that we face an enemy, let alone to name him. Note the frequent use of euphemisms, such as 'the other side,' or 'a potential aggressor.' We have all read dozens of papers by NATO experts that refer to a possible attack on NATO by 'an aggressor,' alluding perhaps to some fairy tale creature like Rumpelstiltskin. Note, also, how loudly President Reagan was criticized for calling the thing by its name. Yes, there is an empire—the only empire left. And yes, this empire is assuredly not benign.

Grafted onto the czarist tradition of imperial expansion, Lenin, Stalin and their heirs seized every opportunity to expand the empire under Moscow's control. Lenin created much of the ideology, institutions and techniques of the system we are now confronting as our enemy. That system is characterized by a self-perpetuating, centralized monopoly of power, by the expert use of violence to maintain this monopoly and to expand its reach and by the steady accumulation of military strength to back up and consolidate the expansion.

While containment has succeeded in Europe and on the Korean peninsula, it has failed elsewhere. In many parts of Asia, Africa and the Caribbean region the Soviet Union has acquired military outposts as well as de facto colonies.

While NATO and Warsaw Pact forces have never fought each other, Soviet-supported Cuban forces are now fighting in Nicaragua and Angola. The Soviet-backed Vietnamese are fighting in Cambodia. And in Afghanistan Soviet forces will soon have been fighting twice as long as they fought Hitler's Wehrmacht.

While nuclear weapons have not been used since 1945, the competition in nuclear armaments has never ceased.

As if oblivious to such constant change, the psyche of our Alliance remains oriented toward a different world. It yearns for a world of stable, tranquil boundaries that peacefully contain the Soviet empire; a world in which the military competition has been arrested and where a stable balance of forces deters aggression; a world fixed in equilibrium by a network of East-West agreements. Such notions of stability have become woven into the fabric of our strategic consciousness. For many people in the West, in fact, the word 'stability' sums up the strategic goal of our Alliance.

To develop a strategy, however, it is necessary to do more than set ultimate goals. A course to these goals must be charted and pursued, through obstacles and opposition. It is necessary sometimes to take the enemy into consideration. We need to recognize the nature of the competition that is being forced upon us.

Our Alliance must learn to compete more effectively in three arenas: in the geo-strategic one, in military forces and in the technologic and economic arena.

For the geo-strategic arena, we must guard against an overly Euro-centric view. Our successful defense of the Central Front must not be allowed to suffer the fate of the Maginot Line. Note how the situation on our Southern Front—in the Mediterranean region—has deteriorated since the Alliance was created. In the 1960s, the ratio of ship days between the United States and the Soviet navy was four to one in the US favor; today it is one-and-a-half to one in the Soviet favor. Wheelus in Libya was an American base until 1969; and there were no Soviet bases on the Red Sea, as there are today in Aden and Ethiopia.

We must also note the changes on another 'southern front' of NATO: the Caribbean region. In the 1950s, US military planners faced no military threat from that region. Today, Cuba's military capabilities and its Soviet installations would pose a serious threat in time of war. The hostile military assets on Cuba could be used to cut critical sea lanes to Europe. And on the American mainland the military buildup in Nicaragua,

USAFE medics (*above*) check a patient's IV aboard a cavernous Medevac aircraft during maneuvers in Europe. Practice makes perfect, and all NATO forces medics certainly get their share of the action (*at right*) come maneuvers time.

with its growing Cuban involvement, poses an even more serious danger. Today, the United States still enjoys an open, unarmed border to the south, and our treaty commitments in Latin America are not militarily demanding. There is now no military front in Central America, unlike in Korea and Europe. But if the United States should have to divert military resources to contain a 'second Cuba' on the American mainland, our Central Front in Europe would indeed have been outflanked.

The global arms balance between East and West is another arena for competition. I won't dwell on the declining US advantage from 1960 until 1980 in nuclear arms. You know these facts all too well. Instead I want to make a broader point. In our search for stability, we assumed the Soviet leaders would settle for nuclear parity, and we complacently expected that the arms competition could easily be brought to a stable resting point. In fact, we invited the Soviet Union to build up to parity in those arms where we had an advantage; but we did not seek to achieve parity in areas where they had an advantage, misled by our faith in the universal attraction of 'stability.' On the contrary, we invited the Soviet military planners to surpass us.

We need change, not to sweep aside the essential values of our Alliance, but to protect them. We need change to preserve the viability of such basic strategic ideas as: the primacy of deterrence, the Alliance's territorial inviolability, effective burden-sharing and the concept of Flexible Response.

Let me give you a few illustrations of specific cases; there are many more that should be addressed.

Consider the current NATO effort to exploit what we have come to call 'Emerging Technologies' for enhancing our conventional forces. In order to succeed, this highly promising effort requires a dynamic sense of competition. If we wish to rely on our technological advantages, we must see to it that we actually maintain a technological advantage. Hence, every ally must lend strong support to COCOM. Hence, we should not too readily impose restrictions on our militarily relevant research and testing. We cannot have, in military technology, both East-West stability and a continuing NATO advantage.

Forward defense close to the Alliance's borders remains a political and strategic imperative. How are we to maintain such a forward defense? The nature of the terrain over which the enemy forces would seek to advance, of course, affects the ease (or difficulties) of our forward defense. And the obstacles

of terrain are not only the work of God, but can also be created by man—as Maréchal Vauban and André Maginot have demonstrated. There are ways to enhance the contribution of natural or artificial terrain features to NATO's forward defense, on the Central Front and elsewhere. Specific proposals to this end obviously have to be carefully assessed. Even before the Flexible Response concept was adopted in 1967, and certainly since then, NATO has pursued a capability to attack Warsaw Pact follow-on forces deep in the enemy's rear. In recent years, NATO's military experts have made great strides in developing promising tactics and exploiting new technologies for this purpose. Yet, bureaucratic fences have anxiously been erected around the concept of attacking follow-on forces. In particular, all proposals for forward maneuver operations that could complement these attacks on follow-on forces are immediately placed on that Index of Prohibited Ideas. The Index protects what I like to call the 'dogma of immaculate aggression.' This dogma holds that our enemy, after launching a full-scale attack into our territory, would remain immaculate of

any sin. Hence, our ground forces would have to keep respecting the entire border between NATO and the Warsaw Pact, even though enemy forces would be pouring across this border into our territory.

The over 100 million Europeans living between NATO's Central Front and the Western borders of the Soviet Union do not support Moscow's imperial ambitions, as they have shown repeatedly at great risk to themselves. Recall the Prague Spring, the Solidarity days in Poland. We should not build our tactics and strategy on the assumption that the peoples of eastern Europe would inevitably support a Soviet war of aggression, because they would have no choice. To rely on this assumption we would risk making it a self-fulfilling prediction. Instead, we should think how we might create possibilities of choice—opportunities for these people to help restore the peace, before Moscow's war would have run its dreadful course. Our plans for deterrence and the defense of the Alliance must not inadvertently lock the peoples of Eastern Europe into Moscow's war machine.

NATO's defense intentness is based on geography and history—with aggressors a stone's throw away from most NATO members, the painful lessons of World War II are indeed engraved upon the European psyche. The European subcontinent is almost claustrophobically cozy, a point which is brought home by the juxtaposition of civilian life and military maneuvers shown *above*.

CHAPTER 4

NATO Military Organization

Prepared by the NATO Information Service

The map *on the opposite page* shows the layout of ACE, aka Allied Command Europe, which is one of three major NATO military commands.

ALLIED COMMAND EUROPE

The North Atlantic Treaty Organization's military command in Europe is Allied Command Europe (ACE). One of three major NATO commands,* ACE exists to safeguard an area that stretches from the northern tip of Norway to the eastern border of Turkey. This is nearly two million square kilometers of land and more than three million square kilometers of sea.

Supreme Headquarters Allied Powers Europe (SHAPE), located near the city of Mons, Belgium (about 45 kilometers southeast of Brussels), is the senior ACE headquarters. From SHAPE, the Supreme Allied Commander Europe (SACEUR) directs efforts to unify defense measures, strengthen military forces and plan for their most effective use in an emergency.

*Allied Command Atlantic is responsible for the Atlantic Ocean while Allied Command Channel has the English Channel as its area of responsibility.

At SHAPE and at other ACE headquarters, integrated staffs drawn from the NATO nations work to broaden and improve the military capability of this defensive Alliance. Throughout the ACE area, land, sea and air exercises continually test and develop international teamwork toward achievement of the goals of NATO.

UNITED KINGDOM AIR FORCES

UKAIR is a Major Subordinate Command (MSC) under the Supreme Allied Commander Europe (SACEUR). It was formed in 1975, with headquarters at High Wycombe in Buckinghamshire, 30 miles (50 kilometers) northwest of London. As a regional command within Allied Command Europe, it is unique in that it is essentially a single-service (Royal Air Force), single-nation MSC and has no Principal Subordinate Command.

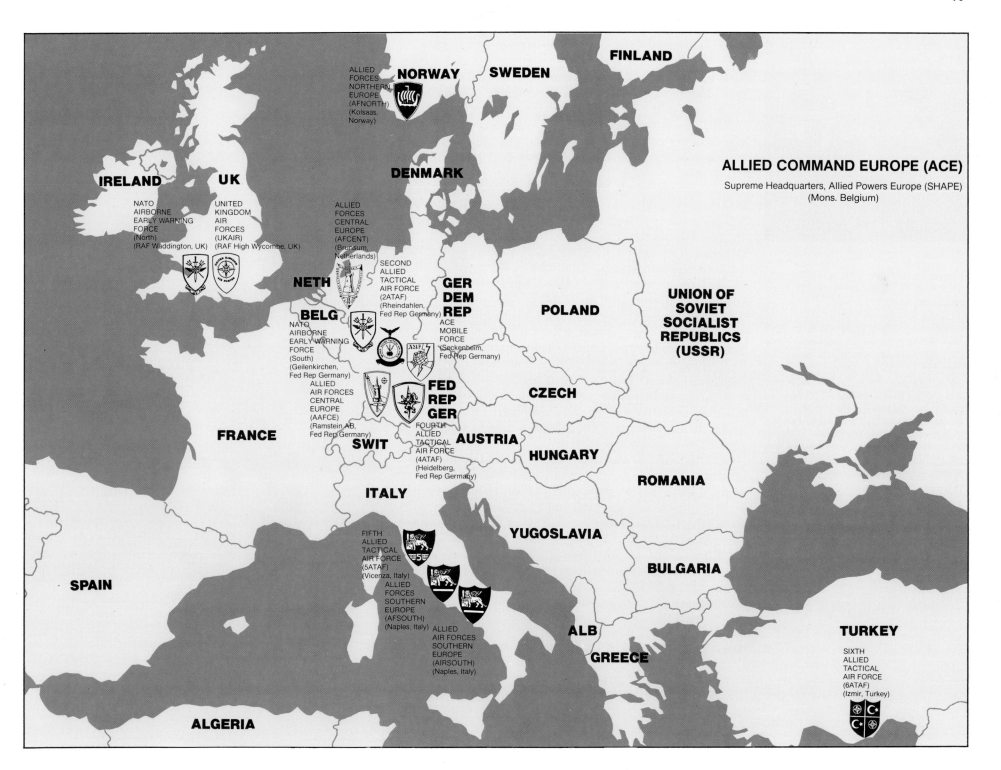

ALLIED COMMAND EUROPE (ACE)

Supreme Headquarters, Allied Powers Europe (SHAPE)
(Mons. Belgium)

NORWAY

SWEDEN

FINLAND

ALLIED FORCES NORTHERN EUROPE (AFNORTH) (Kolsaas, Norway)

DENMARK

IRELAND

UK

NATO AIRBORNE EARLY WARNING FORCE (North) (RAF Waddington, UK)

UNITED KINGDOM AIR FORCES (UKAIR) (RAF High Wycombe, UK)

ALLIED FORCES CENTRAL EUROPE (AFCENT) (Brunsum, Netherlands)

NETH

SECOND ALLIED TACTICAL AIR FORCE (2ATAF) (Rheindahlen, Fed Rep Germany)

GER DEM REP

POLAND

UNION OF SOVIET SOCIALIST REPUBLICS (USSR)

BELG

NATO AIRBORNE EARLY WARNING FORCE (South) (Geilenkirchen, Fed Rep Germany)

ACE MOBILE FORCE (Seckenheim, Fed Rep Germany)

ALLIED AIR FORCES CENTRAL EUROPE (AAFCE) (Ramstein AB, Fed Rep Germany)

FED REP GER

CZECH

FRANCE

SWIT

FOURTH ALLIED TACTICAL AIR FORCE (4ATAF) (Heidelberg, Fed Rep Germany)

AUSTRIA

HUNGARY

ROMANIA

ITALY

SPAIN

FIFTH ALLIED TACTICAL AIR FORCE (5ATAF) (Vicenza, Italy)

ALLIED FORCES SOUTHERN EUROPE (AFSOUTH) (Naples, Italy)

ALLIED AIR FORCES SOUTHERN EUROPE (AIRSOUTH) (Naples, Italy)

YUGOSLAVIA

BULGARIA

ALB

GREECE

TURKEY

SIXTH ALLIED TACTICAL AIR FORCE (6ATAF) (Izmir, Turkey)

ALGERIA

Above: **An RAF Tornado patrols the British Coast, ready to cross the Channel should the necessity arise.**

In the foreground, *opposite,* is an RAF Avro AEW2 Shackleton (Airborne Early Warning) aircraft, which has been 'the guardian of Western Airspace' for some years; its successor in the RAF AEW role was the Hawker-Siddeley AEW3 Nimrod (in the background), aka 'the Pregnant Comet,' which is faster and longer-ranging than the Shackleton. The Nimrod will itself soon be replaced by the Boeing E-3 AWACS such as currently serves in the US Air Force, as well as in Luxembourg markings (see pages 4-5).

Shackletons once served as marine reconnaissance and anti-submarine warfare patrol planes, and still serve in the AEW role.

For its frontline forces, the command draws on most of the home-based operational air resources of the United Kingdom. It is a genuinely multirole command, spanning all of the functions of air power—strike/attack, air defense, reconnaissance and air transport. These frontline resources are provided to SACEUR by three subordinate Royal Air Force formations— No 1 Group (strike/attack), No 11 Group (air defense) and No 38 Group (Offensive Support, Support Helicopters and Air Transport).

Since adoption of the NATO concept of Flexible Response, the United Kingdom has become a major base for offensive, defensive and reinforcement operations, and the security of this base has, therefore, assumed increasing importance. The Commander-in-Chief United Kingdom Air Forces (CINCU-KAIR) is responsible to SACEUR for the air defense of Britain and for protecting the United Kingdom Air Defense Region (UKADR) against air attack.

Stretching some 1200 miles from north to south, the region sits astride the main air and sea reinforcement routes from North America and the United Kingdom to mainland Europe. To carry out this mission, CINCUKAIR employs Phantom and Lightning fighters, Victor air-to-air refuelling tankers, Shackleton Airborne Early Warning (AEW) aircraft (soon to be replaced by the AEW version of the Nimrod), Bloodhound and Rapier surface-to-air missiles and the extensive UK ground radar control and reporting system.

CINCUKAIR is also required by SACEUR to provide combat-ready air forces for employment within Allied Command Europe and to participate, on order, in SACEUR's nuclear programs. To meet these responsibilities, CINCUKAIR provides Vulcan and Buccaneer squadrons (soon to be replaced by the Tornado) in the strike/attack role.

UK-based Harrier and Jaguar offensive support aircraft and Puma and Chinook helicopters are used to reinforce the mainland regions of ACE. The command's air transport force of Hercules and VC10 aircraft is also available for NATO operations.

NATO AIRBORNE EARLY WARNING FORCE

The NAEW Force was created in January 1980. The NAEW Force Command (the Force's headquarters) was granted full status as a major NATO headquarters by the Defense Planning Committee on 17 October 1980. Commander NAEW Force is currently a US Air Force major-general, his

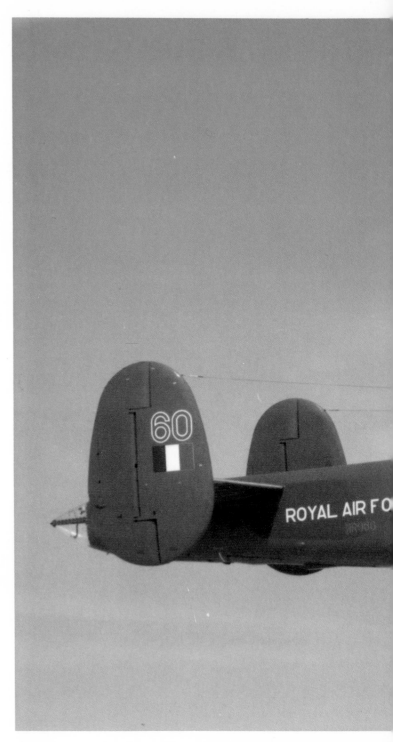

At right: **Inside a USAF E-3A aircraft it boils down to this: the operator scans a sector for bogeys, friendlies and interesting visitors, vectoring fighters under his control to investigate and kill the former. Compare the map shown on this screen to the map on page 73 of this text.**

deputy being a Royal Air Force air commodore. The command is colocated with Supreme Headquarters Allied Powers Europe at Casteau, Belgium.

The operational units of the NAEW Force will be comprised of 18 Boeing E-3A aircraft plus 11 MK 3 Nimrods made by British Aerospace. The Nimrods, which constitute the United Kingdom's contribution to the program, will be manned by RAF personnel, while the E-3As will be manned by mixed crews from 11 of NATO's 16 nations (Belgium, Canada, Denmark, FRG, Greece, Italy, The Netherlands, Norway, Portugal, Turkey and the United States). The E-3A component is the only multinational integrated operational force in the Atlantic Alliance.

The Force's aircraft will have two main operating bases and a number of forward operating bases and locations. The E-3A squadrons will be stationed at Geilenkirchen, FRG and the

Left: The Boeing E-3A Sentry AWACS surveillance system is equipped with Westinghouse pulse-doppler radar, which dome is very evident—atop its stilts on the AWACS' back. The AWACS, with its very sensitive eyes and ears, can manage a large number of combat aircraft over a wide geographic area, and is considered essential to NATO's defense preparations.

Above: Two members of the 17-man AWACS crew check their technical data before boarding the aircraft (behind them). Note the 'NATO (compass rose) OTAN' palindromic command logo on the aircraft's side, near the door. OTAN is actually the French acronym for NATO.

Nimrod squadrons at Waddington, UK. The forward operating bases and locations will be in Turkey, Greece, Norway, Italy and the UK. The E-3A component was activated in June 1982, and the Nimrods will become operational in the near future.

The mission of the NAEW Force is essentially air surveillance of NATO territory in Europe. Flying just behind the border between NATO and the Warsaw Pact, the Force's aircraft will also be able to *see* deep into the potential enemy's territory and will provide communications support for various air operations. The airborne radar systems are interoperable with friendly land and naval forces, and there is a communications capability with both ground-based commanders and naval units at sea.

The AEW radars to be employed in the E-3A and Nimrod have the ability to detect and track enemy aircraft operating at low altitudes over all types of terrain, and to identify and give direction to friendly aircraft operating in the same area. In addition, a 'maritime mode' allows detection of enemy shipping and monitoring of its movements. The mobility of the NAEW Force allows aircraft to be deployed rapidly to wherever needed. This mobility, coupled with the aircraft's ability to direct fighter aircraft for its own defense, makes AEW radar far less vulnerable to attack than ground-based radars.

ALLIED FORCES CENTRAL EUROPE

AFCENT is one of the four Major Subordinate Commands under the Supreme Allied Commander Europe (SACEUR). Headquarters AFCENT was first established at Fontainebleau, France in 1951, then moved to Brunssum, The Netherlands in March 1967 when France withdrew from the integrated military structure of the NATO Alliance.

Commander-in-Chief AFCENT (CINCENT) is responsible for the defense of the Central Region of Allied Command Europe, which extends from the North Sea and the Elbe River to the borders of Austria and Switzerland.

Supporting CINCENT are three Principal Subordinate Commands:

1) HQ Northern Army Group (NORTHAG) at Moenchengladbach, Federal Republic of Germany (FRG);

2) HQ Central Army Group (CENTAG) at Heidelberg, FRG;

3) HQ Allied Air Forces Central Europe (AAFCE) at Ramstein Air Base, FRG.

AAFCE has operational control, in turn, of two Allied Tactical Air Forces (ATAFs)—the Second ATAF and the Fourth ATAF.

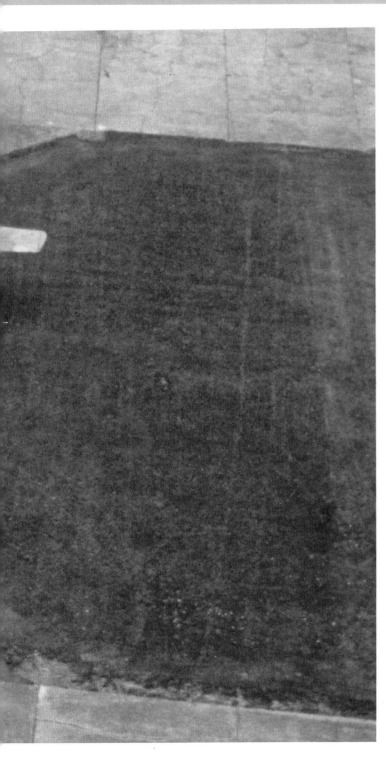

AAFCE was set up in 1974 to improve the effective employment of air resources in the Allied Command Europe (ACE) Central Region. This command is one of the Principal Subordinate Commands under ACE's Major Subordinate Command, AFCENT.

The multinational headquarters, located at Ramstein Air Base, Federal Republic of Germany (FRG), is staffed by personnel from six NATO nations (Belgium, Canada, The Netherlands, the United Kingdom and the United States).

Exercising operational command over the Second and Fourth Allied Tactical Air Forces (TWO- and FOURATAF), Commander Allied Air Forces Central Europe (COMAAFCE) has the mission of directing the integrated employment of Central Region air resources in accordance with the directives of the Commander-in-Chief Allied Forces Central Europe (CINCENT). In other terms, COMAAFCE is responsible for deterring air aggression, countering it if aggression occurs, and maintaining the integrity and security of his area of responsibility, which geographically corresponds with the AFCENT area.

Resources available include some 1500 tactical aircraft and both an offensive and defensive missile force capability. An advanced-design radar system performs warning and control functions, to meet the quick reaction requirements of defense today.

The 'command-forces'—comprising the integrated air defense system—are placed under COMAAFCE's authority in peacetime, while the 'assigned forces' will come under his command as soon as the appropriate political decision is made.

HQ AAFCE peacetime functions include establishing common air doctrines; assessing the threat; determining policies and plans; standardizing procedures, tactics and training; and carrying out exercises, special training programs and flying meets.

The Second Allied Tactical Air Force (TWOATAF) is part of the NATO forces in the Central Region and is subordinate to headquarters, Allied Air Forces Central Europe.

The Commander, TWOATAF is an Air Marshal (Three-Star-Rank) from the United Kingdom Royal Air Force who, in peacetime, is also Commander-in-Chief, Royal Air Force Germany. The TWOATAF headquarters is located at Rheindahlen near Moenchengladbach, Federal Republic of Germany (FRG). Its area of responsibility covers Germany from the German-Danish border in the north down to a Bonn-Kassel

USAFE transport: A Lockheed C-130 Hercules and a Boeing CH-47 Chinook (*opposite*) 'battlefield mobility' helicopter sit on the pavement of a forward field near Wurzburg, West Germany.

Above: A USAFE Fairchild Republic A-10 Warthog awaits orders to fly during war games in Central Europe. The Warthog, built to bust tanks, is homely but effective.

fense forces within the TWOATAF area which are normally assigned to NATO. In support of air defense fighters and missiles during peacetime, there is assigned the NATO Air Defense Ground Environment System (NADGE) consisting of fixed and mobile early warning radars. The low level reporting system (LLRS) completes the surveillance of TWOATAF's air space.

Additionally, TWOATAF is responsible for preparing and coordinating plans and training crews to conduct offensive operations. Modern weapons systems are at the disposal of TWOATAF aircraft and missile personnel to accomplish air defense and offensive operations.

In order to meet the unit's various tasks, air forces from Belgium, the FRG, The Netherlands, United Kingdom and the United States have been assigned to the allied air command.

Headquarters, Fourth Allied Tactical Air Force (FOURATAF) is a component of Allied Air Forces Central Europe. FOURATAF's basic mission is to help secure the NATO air space of Central Europe, achieve and maintain air superiority, destroy enemy forces and provide air support to Army units in its region. The unit also has to obtain tactical information facilitating future engagement of targets and determine the effectiveness of offensive operations.

The FOURATAF area of responsibility comprises a surface of 90,000 square kilometers and a population of approximately 29 million people. In the east, its borders touch those of the Inner German Border and Czechoslovakia; in the south, it borders on Austria and Switzerland. In the west FOURATAF's area bounds the territory of France and includes Luxembourg and part of Belgium. The northern border is marked by the southern border of Headquarters TWOATAF.

FOURATAF is a tri-national force, composed of American, Canadian and German air forces. The three nations appoint air force personnel of all ranks to man the headquarters staff and contribute parts of their air forces to the organization. These forces come under operational control of Headquarters, FOURATAF in the event of an emergency.

FOURATAF shares its area of responsibility with CENTAG—NATO's Central Army Group—also located at Heidelberg, Federal Republic of Germany. For these ground forces the formations of FOURATAF provide the air shield. In fact, FOURATAF's mission is 'to employ its forces in conjunction with those of CENTAG, to maintain the integrity and security of the FOURATAF and CENTAG area, and to provide support as directed to TWOATAF and FIVEATAF.'

Above: A Luftwaffe commander (in black) and a USAF Hercules pilot confer before a tactical airlift exercise in the Federal Republic of Germany.

Opposite: A potpourri of AFCENT's hottest combat aircraft (clockwise from lower left): a USAFE F-16 Falcon; a Luftwaffe F-104 Starfighter; a USAFE F-15 Eagle; a Luftwaffe F.2 Tornado; and a Luftwaffe Alpha Jet.

line in the south, and part of the North Sea, Belgium and The Netherlands.

One of TWOATAF's most important tasks is 'round-the-clock' surveillance of assigned air space with a highly trained alert force of aircraft and missile squadrons able to respond in short notice. Because his air defense responsibility covers both peace and war, the TWOATAF commander has operational control in peacetime of integrated NATO Air Defense Forces. These elements include those land and naval air de-

ALLIED FORCES SOUTHERN EUROPE

The Southern Region is the largest of Allied Command Europe's (ACE's) four military regions, covering an area of approximately one-and-one-half million square miles. AFSOUTH is the ACE Major Subordinate Command with the responsibility for defending this region. Operating under the Commander-in-Chief AFSOUTH (CINCSOUTH), a four-star United States admiral, are five Primary Subordinate Commands (PSCs).

1) Allied Air Forces Southern Europe (AIRSOUTH), headquartered at Naples, Italy;

2) Allied Land Forces Southern Europe (LANDSOUTH), headquartered at Verona, Italy;

3) Allied Land Forces Southeastern Europe (LANDSOUTHEAST), headquartered at Izmir, Turkey;

4) Allied Naval Forces Southern Europe (NAVSOUTH), headquartered on Nisida Island in the Bay of Naples, Italy;

5) Naval Striking and Support Forces Southern Europe (STRIKFORSOUTH), headquartered aboard the USS *Puget Sound* (AD-38), homeported at Gaeta, Italy.

AFSOUTH's area of responsibility covers Italy, Greece, Turkey, the Black Sea and the entire Mediterranean Sea, including the Tyrrhenian, Adriatic, Ionian and Aegean Seas.

AFSOUTH was originally established in June 1951, with headquarters on a US naval warship in the Bay of Naples. AFSOUTH headquarters are now located in the Bagnoli district of Naples, Italy.

AIRSOUTH, headquartered at the Allied Forces Southern Europe (AFSOUTH) Post in the Bagnoli district of Naples, is one of the five Principal Subordinate Commands in Allied Command Europe's Southern Region. Besides the multinational staff at the headquarters, comprised of personnel from Greece, Italy, Turkey, the UK and the US, AIRSOUTH also comprises Allied Tactical Air Forces (ATAFs) at Vicenza, Italy (Fifth ATAF) and Izmir, Turkey (Sixth ATAF), each of which exercises unified control of existing allied air forces in their respective countries. Commander AIRSOUTH (COMAIRSOUTH) is a three-star USAF general.

AIRSOUTH's area of responsibility is the airspace over the Southern Region, ie the mainland areas and island possessions of Italy, Greece and Turkey, including Sardinia, Sicily, Crete, etc. In all, AIRSOUTH must defend a 3600 kilometer (2000 mile) border, stretching from the Italian Alps to eastern Turkey.

Opposite: Italian troops before boarding a C-130 Hercules troop transport (background) in an AFSOUTH tactical exercise.

At left is an Italian Air Force example of the Fiat-built F-104S Starfighter variant, which is capable of carrying AIM-7 Sparrow AAM (air-to-air) missiles (visible under wings). The F-104S is currently being flown by Italy and Turkey.

An Italian NATO paratrooper (*above*) smiles a camouflaged smile in greeting to his allies of the Western world.

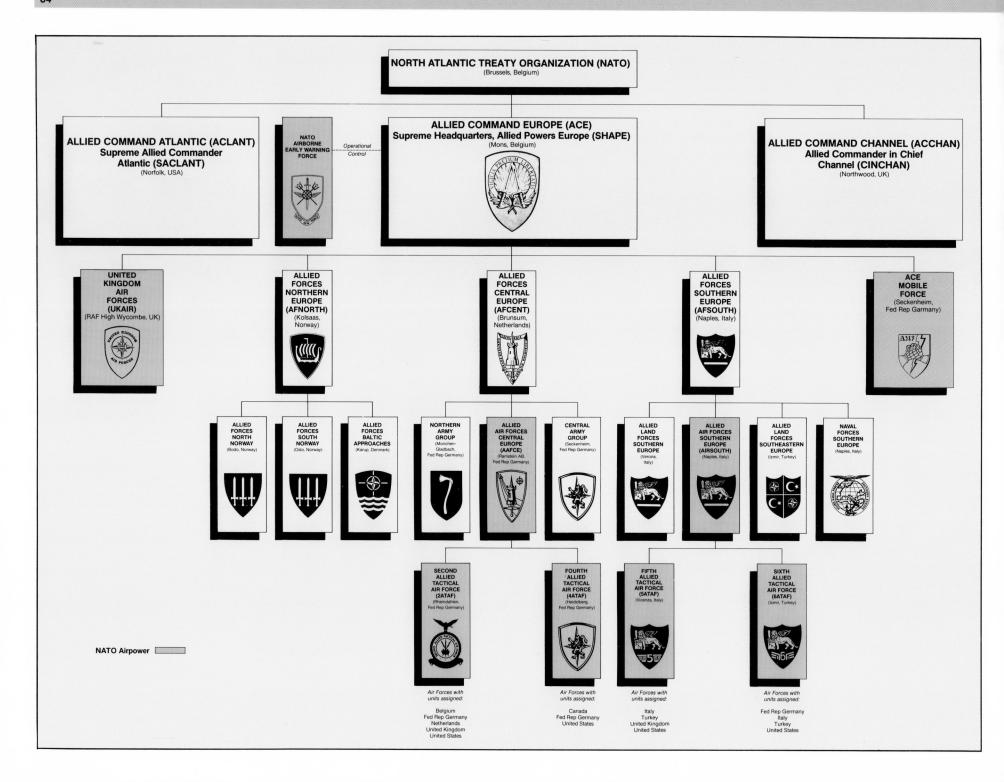

NATO Airpower

AIRSOUTH was established in August 1951 and underwent a number of evolutions until reaching its present structure after the Cyprus conflict in 1974.

To prepare for its wartime mission of conducting the air defense of the Southern Region, the peacetime activities of AIRSOUTH include standardizing training and operating procedures, coordinating the exchange of information and use of facilities between the various countries, and solving the ever-present problems of personnel, equipment, tactics and techniques.

Valuable experience has been gained in this day-to-day international cooperation and association, both at HQ and in the field, during frequent NATO training exercises.

Equipment available to the operational forces under COM-AIRSOUTH control include F1 Mirages, F-4 Phantoms, F-5 Freedom Fighters, Fiat G-91s, A-7 Corsairs and Tornado Multirole Combat Aircraft (MRCAs), plus Nike Hercules and Hawk surface-to-air missiles.

Headquarters, Fifth Allied Tactical Air Force (FIVE-ATAF) was established on 1 January 1956, at Vicenza, Italy, as a subordinate command of Allied Air Forces Southern Europe.

FIVEATAF's area of responsibility includes the Italian peninsula, its islands and adjacent waters. Its primary mission, in case of emergency, is to conduct activities to counter aggression through offensive and defensive operations within the area of responsibility.

In 1962, when the National Air Defense systems were integrated into the overall NATO air defense organization, the Italian air defense forces, facilities and ground environment were placed under NATO operational control. Consequently, the FIVEATAF commander was assigned operational control of these forces and given responsibility for air defense of the entire Italian territory and adjacent waters.

Headquarters, FIVEATAF's main peacetime task is to direct and control air defense assets, develop plans for possible wartime use of forces available, participate in major NATO exercises, and conduct tactical evaluations on the level of combat readiness by its subordinate assigned air units.

FIVEATAF has an integrated staff which includes personnel from the Federal Republic of Germany, Italy, Turkey and the United States.

The bulk of forces assigned to FIVEATAF is represented by Italian and US Air Force units including offensive, defensive and reconnaissance fighter squadrons, surface-to-air missiles and an air defense ground environment.

The Sixth Allied Tactical Air Force (SIXATAF) is a component of Allied Air Forces Southern Europe. The command was established on 14 October 1953, with its headquarters at Sirinyer Garrison, south of Izmir, Turkey.

SIXATAF has the peacetime mission of providing fulltime air defense of Turkey. In addition to its air defense role, the headquarters serves as a planning and advisory agency and conducts tactical evaluations of assigned units on a regular basis to ensure that a high state of readiness is maintained.

SIXATAF's wartime mission is to counter aggression by conducting air operations in defense of Turkey. Maintaining its air defense role, SIXATAF would also provide tactical air support to NATO naval and land forces.

In the event of war in the southeastern region, the SIX-ATAF commander would assume operational control, following national approval, of two Turkish tactical air forces (TAF). These are the First TAF, headquartered at Eskisehir (east of Istanbul), and the Second TAF, located at Diyarbakir in southeastern Turkey. Both TAFs include several types of aircraft squadrons equipped and trained to conduct counter air, close air support, air interdiction, reconnaissance and air defense operations.

The international staff of SIXATAF headquarters includes personnel from Italy, Turkey, the United Kingdom and the United States.

SIXATAF's geographic area of responsibility is one of the largest of any allied tactical air force command in NATO.

Above: A Turkish F-4 Phantom. The Phantom is a two-seater, replete with pilot and weapons systems operator, or GIB—'Guy In Back.' The GIB sits in the 'pit,' so named for the lack of visibility provided for the rear man in the F-104.

Opposite: The emblems and insignia of the various NATO groups, presented hierarchically in order of major command.

CHAPTER 5

An Overview of USAFE Airpower

Prepared by USAFE Public Affairs

Opposite: **This air-to-air photograph was taken during the 1982 Reforger (Return of Forces to Germany)/Crested Cap II combined forces military maneuvers in West Germany; these two USAFE F-15 Eagles are equipped with belly tanks for extra range as they cruise the German Federal Republic's North Sea coast.**

The United States Air Forces in Europe (USAFE), with headquarters at Ramstein Air Base, West Germany, is a major command of the US Air Force. It is also the air component of the United States European Command, one of the Department of Defense's unified commands.

USAFE originated as the VIII Fighter Command of the Eighth Air Force in 1942 whose primary role was to conduct heavy bombardment missions against the European continent during World War II. In January 1944, the Eighth Air Force and the newly-formed Fifteenth Air Force, organized in Italy to attack Nazi territory from the south, were redesignated the United States Strategic Air Forces in Europe, responsible for directing operations in Europe and the Middle East. Subordinate units included the VIII Fighter Command and the VIII Bomber Command. On 7 August 1945, after the Eighth Air Force and VIII Bomber Command were transferred to the Pacific for operations against Japan, the VIII Fighter Command officially became the United States Air Forces in Europe.

The new command shared occupation duties with the US Army in the American zones in West Germany and Austria. It disarmed remnants of the German Luftwaffe and disposed of vast quantities of US war materials. By 1947, these tasks were nearly completed and, as the command's strength dwindled, USAFE became mostly an administrative force.

When the Soviets blockaded West Berlin in June 1948, the West answered with the Berlin Airlift. United States Air Forces in Europe airlifted food, fuel and medical supplies to the city with the aid of the US Navy and the British Royal Air Force. During the 15-month airlift operation, allied aircraft flew 277,264 missions, delivering 2,326,204 tons of supplies to Berlin. To give armed support to these flights, USAFE activated the Third Air Division in England. As a direct consequence of the Berlin blockade, USAFE expanded its aircraft force with 75 new F-80 jet fighters.

With the formation of the North Atlantic Treaty Organization in 1949, the United States, as a member, was committed

to assist in the defense of Western Europe. As a result, USAFE again strengthened its airpower in Europe.

By the end of 1951, rights were granted for the construction of several bases in France. Airfield sites in the French Occupation Zone of Germany, west of the Rhine River, were also made available. Combat units deployed from the United States to West Germany, France, United Kingdom and the Netherlands. Eventually, the command was assigned units and responsibilities in French Morocco, Libya, Saudi Arabia, Greece, Turkey, Italy and Spain.

Many organizational changes took place because of these increased responsibilities. In 1951, USAFE discontinued the Third Air Division and activated the Third Air Force. The Seventeenth Air Force, activated in French Morocco in 1953, moved to Libya in 1956 and then relocated to West Germany in 1959. The United States Logistics Group (TUSLOG) was organized in Turkey in 1955, becoming the primary support element in Turkey for all US military forces. In 1966, the Sixteenth Air Force in Spain was assigned to USAFE.

The command underwent a major reorganization when France withdrew from military participation in NATO, requiring all foreign troops to leave France by April 1967. Nine major bases and 78 smaller installations in France were closed, and personnel and materiel were relocated to the United Kingdom, West Germany and the United States.

Changes continued through the early 1970s. The Seventeenth Air Force was moved from Ramstein Air Base to Sembach Air Base, West Germany in 1972. Headquarters USAFE was relocated from Lindsey Air Station, West Germany to Ramstein Air Base in March 1973, and on 28 June 1974, NATO's Allied Air Forces Central Europe (AAFCE) was established at Ramstein. The USAFE commander in chief was then assigned dual responsibilities as commander of AAFCE.

Improvements in the command's weapon systems began in the early 1970s and continue today. With the addition of more advanced aircraft, the command has strengthened its capability to achieve air superiority and support allied ground forces to overcome enemy aggression. In addition to state-of-the-art

MAC/USAFE airlift—then and now: *Opposite:* A pair of C-82 troop carriers of the type that saw extensive service in the years immediately after World War II and helped out, ferrying supplies, with the Berlin Airlift of the late forties; and *above* a MAC C-130 Hercules transport comes in for a landing on European soil.

Lockheed-built, the Hercules is big (it can carry approximately 85,000 pounds of payload), versatile (it can carry personnel and supplies, has been outfitted as a devastating gunship in the Vietnam War and has been used as an electronic equipment test platform) and reliable (it can go anywhere, practically, in any kind of weather, and 'start every time'). The 'Herc' serves with almost every NATO power, making it the current standard transport for men and supplies.

aircraft, USAFE now has a ground launched cruise missile capability. This system complements the US Army Pershing II missile to offset the Soviet missile build-up. The GLCMs were introduced into USAFE as a result of the 1979 NATO ministers' dual-track intermediate-range nuclear force decision.

Through realignment and reconfiguration of its forces, USAFE is a streamlined, tightly managed, NATO-committed force possessing a greatly improved combat readiness posture.

In peacetime, the command trains and equips US Air Force units pledged to NATO. Under wartime conditions, its tactical fighters, fighter-bombers and reconnaissance aircraft come under the operational command of NATO. The command's weapon systems are ready for close air support, air interdiction, air defense, reconnaissance operations and support of maritime operations. Strategic and tactical airlift are provided under a joint USAFE-Military Airlift Command agreement.

In fulfilling its NATO responsibilities, the command maintains combat-ready units dispersed in an area from Great Britain to Turkey. It provides fighter, reconnaissance and airlift support for all NATO exercises conducted in the Western European area and assists allied air forces with developing their combat capabilities.

As a component of the United States European Command, a unified command composed of US military forces, USAFE supports US military plans and operations in western Europe, the Mediterranean, the Middle East and portions of Africa.

Most of USAFE's 30 major operational bases, its 20 wings, its approximately 725 aircraft and its more than 69,000 US Air Force military and civilian personnel are concentrated in Western Europe. Major units are maintained in the United Kingdom, West Germany, Greece, Italy, the Netherlands, Spain, Belgium and Turkey.

About 33,000 more Air Force personnel stationed throughout the command are assigned to other major commands including MAC, the Strategic Air Command, the Air Force Communications Command and the Electronic Security Command.

The command is divided into three numbered air forces:

The Third Air Force, with headquarters at Royal Air Force Station Mildenhall, England, provides support for Air Force personnel in England. The Third Air Force has eight bases under its direction.

• RAF Alconbury (10th Tactical Reconnaissance Wing). The wing has one squadron of RF-4C's and one squadron of F-5E's. The 17th Reconnaissance Wing, a SAC unit, is equipped with one squadron of TR-1As.

Opposite: A USAFE F-15 Eagle of the 17th AF's 32nd TFS at Camp New Amsterdam, Soesterberg, the Netherlands. Capable of 1653 mph with four AIM-7 Sparrow AAMs strapped on, the F-15 Eagle is a fast, maneuverable and very deadly fighting plane.

Built as an 'Air Superiority' fighter, the Eagle is the rock 'em, sock 'em MiG buster of the USAFE skies. Every young USAF fighter jock wants one, (and wants one bad) especially in the European theater—where the training is intense, for that's where the action is likely to get 'real hot, real fast'—if it gets hot anywhere. *Above: Rara avis:* the F-15 Eagle.

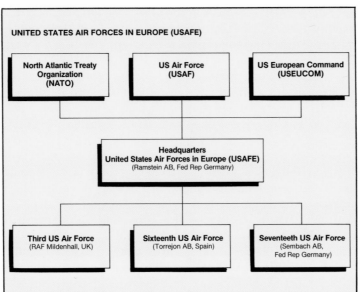

UNITED STATES AIR FORCES IN EUROPE (USAFE)

North Atlantic Treaty Organization (NATO)	US Air Force (USAF)	US European Command (USEUCOM)

**Headquarters
United States Air Forces in Europe (USAFE)**
(Ramstein AB, Fed Rep Germany)

Third US Air Force (RAF Mildenhall, UK)	Sixteenth US Air Force (Torrejon AB, Spain)	Seventeeth US Air Force (Sembach AB, Fed Rep Germany)

Above: The USAFE insignia; *above right:* a chart of the USAFE organization; *opposite:* a map of USAFE organizational and operational sites.

• RAF Upper Heyford (20th Tactical Fighter Wing). Three squadrons of F-111E's and one squadron of EF-111A's are assigned to the base.
• RAF Lakenheath (48th Tactical Fighter Wing). The wing is comprised of four squadrons of F-111F's.
• RAF Bentwaters/RAF Woodbridge (81st Tactical Fighter Wing). The wing is equipped with six squadrons of A-10s. The 67th Aerospace Rescue and Recovery Squadron (MAC) at RAF Woodbridge operates HH-53 helicopters and HC-130s.
• RAF Greenham Common (501st Tactical Missile Wing). The wing maintains and operates BGM-109 ground launched cruise missiles.
• RAF Mildenhall (513th Tactical Airlift Wing). This 'Gateway to the United Kingdom' is the aerial port of entry for the majority of US military members and their families assigned to the United Kingdom. The wing operates four EC-135s, provides support for rotational MAC C-130s and SAC KC-135s and KC-10s, and supports additional MAC aircraft.
• RAF Chicksands (7274th Air Base Group). The group provides support for the 6950th Electronic Security Group.
• RAF Fairford (7020th Air Base Group). Supports rotational SAC KC-135 Stratotankers.

The Sixteenth Air Force, with headquarters at Torrejon Air Base, Spain, directs the command's assets in the Mediterranean area. Ten bases come under its supervision.

• Incirlik Air Base, Turkey (39th Tactical Group). The primary mission of the group is to prepare for and conduct air support and training operations.
• Ankara Air Station, Turkey (7217th Air Base Group). Logistic support is provided to the Joint United States Military Mission for Aid to Turkey and The United States Logistics Group.
• Izmir Air Station, Turkey (7241st Air Base Group). The group provides logistic support to NATO units.
• Aviano Air Base, Italy (40th Tactical Group). The group exercises command and control of any weapon systems assigned at Aviano Air Base.
• Comiso Air Station, Italy (487th Tactical Missile Wing). The wing maintains and operates BGM-109 ground launched cruise missiles.
• San Vito Air Station, Italy (7275th Air Base Group). The unit supports the 6917th Electronic Security Group and the 2113th Electronic Security Squadron.
• Torrejon Air Base, Spain (401st Tactical Fighter Wing). The wing has three squadrons of F-16s assigned.
• Zaragoza Air Base, Spain (406th Tactical Fighter Training Wing). The unit provides weapons training facilities and support for tactical aircraft deploying to the base from throughout the command.
• Hellenikon Air Base, Greece (7206th Air Base Group). The group provides support and command and control to its subordinate units as well as administrative and logistical support for United States units and organizations throughout Greece, the Middle East, the Eastern Mediterranean and parts of Africa.
• Iraklion Air Station, Greece (7276th Air Base Group). The organization provides administrative and logistical support to the 6931st Electronic Security Squadron.

The Seventeenth Air Force, with headquarters at Sembach Air Base, West Germany, is responsible for the command's tactical units in West Germany, Belgium and the Netherlands. Eleven bases fall under its direction.

• Zweibruecken Air Base, West Germany (26th Tactical Reconnaissance Wing). The wing has one squadron of RF-4s and provides support for C-23A's assigned to the 10th Military Airlift Squadron (MAC) as the airlift element of the European Distribution System.
• Bitburg Air Base, West Germany (36th Tactical Fighter Wing). Three squadrons of F-15s are assigned.
• Hahn Air Base, West Germany (50th Tactical Fighter Wing). The wing is composed of three squadrons of F-16s.

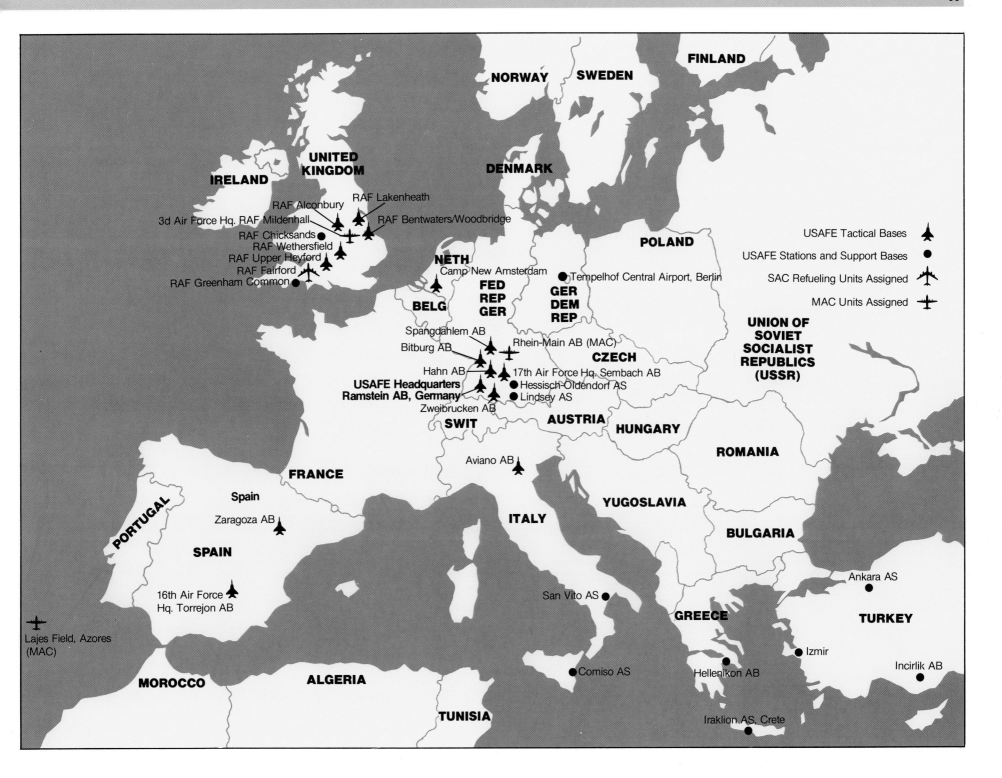

FINLAND

NORWAY SWEDEN

UNITED
KINGDOM

IRELAND DENMARK

RAF Lakenheath

RAF Alconbury

3d Air Force Hq. RAF Mildenhall

RAF Bentwaters/Woodbridge

RAF Chicksands

RAF Wethersfield

NETH

POLAND

RAF Upper Heyford

Camp New Amsterdam

RAF Fairford

Tempelhof Central Airport, Berlin

RAF Greenham Common

FED
REP
GER

GER
DEM
REP

BELG

USAFE Tactical Bases

USAFE Stations and Support Bases

SAC Refueling Units Assigned

MAC Units Assigned

Spangdahlem AB

Rhein-Main AB (MAC)

UNION OF
SOVIET
SOCIALIST
REPUBLICS
(USSR)

Bitburg AB

CZECH

Hahn AB

17th Air Force Hq. Sembach AB

USAFE Headquarters
Ramstein AB, Germany

Hessisch-Oldendorf AS

Lindsey AS

Zweibrucken AB

SWIT

AUSTRIA

HUNGARY

Aviano AB

ROMANIA

FRANCE

YUGOSLAVIA

PORTUGAL

Spain

ITALY

BULGARIA

Zaragoza AB

SPAIN

Ankara AS

16th Air Force
Hq. Torrejon AB

San Vito AS

GREECE

TURKEY

Lajes Field, Azores
(MAC)

Izmir

Comiso AS

Incirlik AB

Hellenikon AB

MOROCCO

ALGERIA

TUNISIA

Iraklion AS, Crete

• Wueschheim Air Station, West Germany (38th Tactical Missile Wing). The wing will maintain and operate BGM-109 ground launched cruise missiles.

• Ramstein Air Base, West Germany (316th Air Division). The air division is responsible for the Kaiserslautern Military Community and two wings—the 86th Tactical Fighter Wing and the 377th Combat Support Wing. The 86th TFW is equipped with two squadrons of F-4Es and is converting to three squadrons of F-16s during 1986. The 377th CSW provides administrative and logistical support for the base.

• Sembach Air Base, West Germany (65th Air Division). The air division has three wings—the 601st Tactical Control Wing and the 66th Electronic Combat Wing at Sembach and the 52nd Tactical Fighter Wing at Spangdahlem Air Base, West Germany. The 601st TCW is responsible for radar control and surveillance of US and allied aircraft involved in both offensive and defensive air operations in central Europe. The wing has one squadron of CH-53s assigned. The 66th ECW provides logistical support to associate units, 53 geographically separated units throughout Europe and flying units which use Sembach Air Base as a forward operating location. It also commands EF-111A aircraft and other electronic warfare systems.

• Spangdahlem Air Base, West Germany (52nd Tactical Fighter Wing). The wing is equipped with three squadrons of F-4E/G's paired into air defense suppression teams.

• Hessisch-Oldendorf Air Station, West Germany (600th Combat Support Squadron). The squadron directs, plans, coordinates and executes command and control for US Air Force aircraft in NATO's Second Allied Tactical Air Force.

• Lindsey Air Station, West Germany (7100th Combat Support Wing). The base provides logistical and administrative support to assigned, attached and associate Air Force units in the area. It supports and administers collocated operating bases and munitions support squadrons throughout the central region.

• Camp New Amsterdam, the Netherlands (32nd Tactical Fighter Squadron). The squadron flies F-15s.

• Florennes Air Base, Belgium (485th Tactical Missile Wing). The wing maintains and operates BGM-109 ground launched cruise missiles.

• Tempelhof Central Airport, Berlin (7350th Air Base Group). The group provides administrative, logistical and security support to assigned, attached and associate units. It reports directly to Headquarters USAFE.

Opposite: Ground crewmen in chemical warfare gear prepare to load Mk-82 'Snakeye' bombs into an A-10 Thunderbolt 'hog (in the background), at Sembach Air Base in West Germany during Exercise UREX 82.

Chemical weaponry is an integral part of the Warsaw pact arsenal, so NATO personnel must be prepared to live and work in an atmosphere that would leave even a native of the planet Jupiter gasping for breath.

On the perimeter of USAFE air bases can be found the humble but very essential ground troop (*above*), guarding the proud Eagles, Falcons and other high tech aircraft from the forces of Earth and gravity—the enemy.

Above: **A pair of USAFE Eagles over the cold Atlantic.**

A front line ground attack tool for USAFE, the Fairchild A-10 Thunderbolt (shown *above right* in Europe) is extremely ugly, but is ugly like a fox—or a Warthog (known to be a wily beast): Nitty-gritty functionality is the key to its 'good looks'—and it looks good to any operational officer, who knows that this beast will fly with half a wing gone, missing one engine and with holes in its sides. It was built to accommodate the massive (longer than a Volkswagen) 30mm GAU-8/A high-velocity, high energy Gatling gun, which fires super dense spent-uranium projectiles to bust tank armor like steel through cardboard. The A-10 also has room for 14,341 lbs of optional gear including bombs, missiles, navigational pods—you name it.

USAFE's aircraft are becoming increasingly modular-electronics oriented; a circuit fails, you pull out the 'black box' in which it's contained and literally pop in a replacement black box for a quicker aircraft repair time—then you take the busted black box to the testing and repair shop (*at right*) where folks like this USAFE sergeant open it up and give it a going over.

Opposite: **A US Air Force Military Airlift Command Sikorsky Super Jolly heavylift helicopter plies the air above a German manor during NATO Central Europe military exercises in 1982.**

The following aircraft are assigned to USAFE: The A-10 Thunderbolt II provides close air support to ground forces. The F-4E Phantom II provides tactical capability for air-to-ground and air-to-air offensive and defensive operations, while the F-4G (Wild Weasel) provides increased survivability to tactical strike forces by seeking out and destroying enemy surface-to-air missile sites. The F-111E/F-111F provide long-range, all-weather, day or night air-to-ground capability, while the EF-111A Raven provides electronic countermeasures support for tactical air forces. The F-15C/F-15D Eagle provides first-line air defense, and the F-5E Tiger II provides dissimilar air combat training. The RF-4C Phantom II provides primary all-weather, day-night reconnaissance. The F-16A/F-16B/F-16C/F-16D Fighting Falcon aircraft provide air-to-air combat and air-to-ground attack capability. Improved munitions give fighter crews an additional capability. Guided weapons have added a new capability to the weapons inventory to counter the growing threat posed by the Soviet Union.

Other aircraft frequently used throughout the command include MAC's UH-1Ns, HC-130s, HH-53s, C-23As, C-130s, C-21As, C-12Fs, C-135Bs, C-141Bs, C-5As and C-9s. The command also hosts SAC's KC-135s, KC-10s, SR-71s and TR-1As. TAC's E-3As (AWACS) also operate in the theater. The CH-53 Super Jolly provides cargo and personnel carrying

A USAFE EF-111 Raven (*at right*) cuts a gracious profile against Central European skies. Based on the F-111 Aardvark, the Raven is a substantially different aircraft, specifically designed for electronic warfare. This USAFE electronic jamming systems aircraft is based at RAF Upper Heyford. The EF-111 is designed for both close-in and stand-off jamming operations and for escorting attack aircraft penetrating enemy airspace; its equipment includes the internally mounted ALQ-99 primary jammer, ALQ-137/ALR-62 self-protection systems and provision for carrying the new ALQ-131 externally.

Below right: An Air Force Reserve/SAC KC-135 tanker refuels one of a pair of TAC F-16s on a typical European deployment exercise. F-16 wing partners wait for their partners to finish refueling as part of their formational agreement, aka 'contract.'

Opposite: An F-4 Phantom of the 526th Tactical Fighter Squadron, 86th TFW, swoops over NATO territory with a complement of four AIM-7 Sparrows and four AIM-9 Sidewinders underwing.

Overleaf: A brace of USAFE F-15s overfly the West German countryside. These Eagles are based at Bitburg, aka 'Fighter Pilot Heaven,' so named for its concentration of top pilots and their hot machines—F-15s.

capability. The EC-135 provides airborne command and control operations for the US European Command.

The command is equipped with the BGM-109G ground launched cruise missile, a highly-survivable, mobile weapon system designed for theater operations in support of NATO.

In addition to its permanent forces in Europe, the command is augmented by active duty Air National Guard and Air Force Reserve units which are committed to NATO in wartime. In the event of mobilization, these units are ready to deploy to Europe on short notice. The personnel assigned to these units are counted as European assets for contingency planning, military exercises and during wartime.

Augmenting squadrons are prepared for rapid deployment to European locations and are ready to support USAFE at any time. The squadrons are rotated overseas periodically for training in the European environment.

Air crews receive regular training in the latest techniques of aerial combat, attack, close air support, reconnaissance and strike tactics relevant to the European theater. Air crew training under poor weather conditions is emphasized throughout the year. Pilots are required to fly in weather conditions which include low cloud ceilings, heavy cloud coverage and long hours of winter darkness.

CHAPTER 6

An Overview of NATO Airpower Today

by Bill Yenne

The US Air Force is the largest air force of any NATO member but USAFE; however, its actual contribution to NATO airpower is slightly smaller than the West German Luftwaffe (over 100,000), with roughly the same number of personnel (over 90,000) as the air forces of France and the UK. Italy comes next with just over 70,000.

NATO's respective air forces have recently been characterized by several important standardization programs. This, beyond a general discussion of their respective sizes, is the most important feature of overall NATO airpower. In the 1960s, the Starfighter program saw Canada, Germany, Belgium, Italy, the Netherlands and Norway (as well as the United States) acquire the F-104 Starfighter as a common first-line, multirole combat aircraft. While not completely successful, the program taught the lessons that paved the way for several important programs that have come into place since the early 1980s. These have included the Tornado, which is now the first line warplane of Germany, Italy and the UK; the F-16 Falcon, that serves in the forefront of the air forces of Belgium, Denmark, Greece, the Netherlands, Norway, Turkey and the United States; and finally, the new F/A-18 Hornet that is in service with Canada, Spain and the US Navy. These three programs account for over a dozen NATO air arms, if one includes the navies of Germany and the United States.

A rough profile of individual NATO air forces aside from the United States is given below. In addition to the combat types mentioned, these air forces maintain varying numbers of training and liaison aircraft. Most also have helicopters, but like the United States, the majority of military helicopters are assigned to the army.

While most NATO air forces have large transports, France, Federal Germany and the UK also each maintain nearly one hundred first line airlifters such as C-130s and C-160s, while France and the UK each maintain aerial refueling aircraft.

THE FEDERAL REPUBLIC OF GERMANY

The Luftwaffe, with over 100,000 personnel, is western Europe's largest air arm. Its aircraft include well over a hundred Tornados and nearly two hundred F-4 Phantoms, with a third of the latter earmarked for reconnaissance. There are still nearly one hundred F-104 Starfighters in the fighter-bomber role, which in turn are augmented by over one hundred Alpha Jet light attack bombers.

The Bundesmarine (navy) maintains about one hundred combat aircraft in the antiship attack and armed reconnaissance roles. These are divided roughly equally between Tornados and Starfighters.

Far opposite: Colonel Reinhardt, Base Commander of Kaufbeurem AFB, Federal Republic of Germany.

These three planes are shown in Luftwaffe livery, respectively, left to right—Phantom, Tornado, Starfighter—*at below left.* All three are capable of high speed and can be used as either fighters or fighter bombers.

The location of this photo is the Messerschmitt-Bolkow-Blohm GmbH plant at Manching, West Germany, where all three were produced under licensing agreements.

At left: The F-4, an unpretty but 'solid' bird, cuts the air above West Germany, wearing Luftwaffe colors.

At left: Luftwaffe Phantoms in formation; Luftwaffe personnel (*above*) have an impromptu conference; a Luftwaffe Tornado equipped with an underbelly-slung MBB MW-1 lateral munitions dispenser is 'pursued' by a Luftwaffe two-seated Starfighter variant (*below*). *Above right:* the Luftwaffe's relationship to NATO; and West German air base locations.

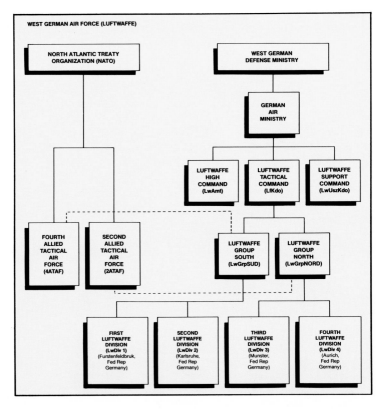

WEST GERMAN AIR FORCE (LUFTWAFFE)

```
┌─────────────────────────┐                    ┌─────────────────────────┐
│ NORTH ATLANTIC TREATY   │                    │   WEST GERMAN           │
│ ORGANIZATION (NATO)     │                    │   DEFENSE MINISTRY      │
└─────────────────────────┘                    └─────────────────────────┘
                                                            │
                                                ┌─────────────────────────┐
                                                │   GERMAN                │
                                                │   AIR                   │
                                                │   MINISTRY              │
                                                └─────────────────────────┘

                        ┌──────────────┐  ┌──────────────┐  ┌──────────────┐
                        │ LUFTWAFFE    │  │ LUFTWAFFE    │  │ LUFTWAFFE    │
                        │ HIGH         │  │ TACTICAL     │  │ SUPPORT      │
                        │ COMMAND      │  │ COMMAND      │  │ COMMAND      │
                        │ (LwAmt)      │  │ (LfKdo)      │  │ (LwUszKdo)   │
                        └──────────────┘  └──────────────┘  └──────────────┘

┌──────────────┐  ┌──────────────┐    ┌──────────────┐  ┌──────────────┐
│ FOURTH       │  │ SECOND       │    │ LUFTWAFFE    │  │ LUFTWAFFE    │
│ ALLIED       │  │ ALLIED       │    │ GROUP        │  │ GROUP        │
│ TACTICAL     │  │ TACTICAL     │    │ SOUTH        │  │ NORTH        │
│ AIR          │  │ AIR          │    │ (LwGrpSUD)   │  │ (LwGrpNORD)  │
│ FORCE        │  │ FORCE        │    └──────────────┘  └──────────────┘
│ (4ATAF)      │  │ (2ATAF)      │
└──────────────┘  └──────────────┘

        ┌──────────────┐  ┌──────────────┐  ┌──────────────┐  ┌──────────────┐
        │ FIRST        │  │ SECOND       │  │ THIRD        │  │ FOURTH       │
        │ LUFTWAFFE    │  │ LUFTWAFFE    │  │ LUFTWAFFE    │  │ LUFTWAFFE    │
        │ DIVISION     │  │ DIVISION     │  │ DIVISION     │  │ DIVISION     │
        │ (LwDiv 1)    │  │ (LwDiv 2)    │  │ (LwDiv 3)    │  │ (LwDiv 4)    │
        │ (Furstenfeld-│  │ (Karlsruhe,  │  │ (Munster,    │  │ (Aurich,     │
        │ bruk, Fed Rep│  │ Fed Rep      │  │ Fed Rep      │  │ Fed Rep      │
        │ Germany)     │  │ Germany)     │  │ Germany)     │  │ Germany)     │
        └──────────────┘  └──────────────┘  └──────────────┘  └──────────────┘
```

L German Air Force (Luftwaffe) Bases
M German Naval Air (Marineflieger) Bases
H German Army Air (Heeresflieger) Bases
S Training Bases (Schule)

A pair of West German Panavia Tornados (*these pages*) fly a tight fighting formation in a practice run above a bucolic setting.

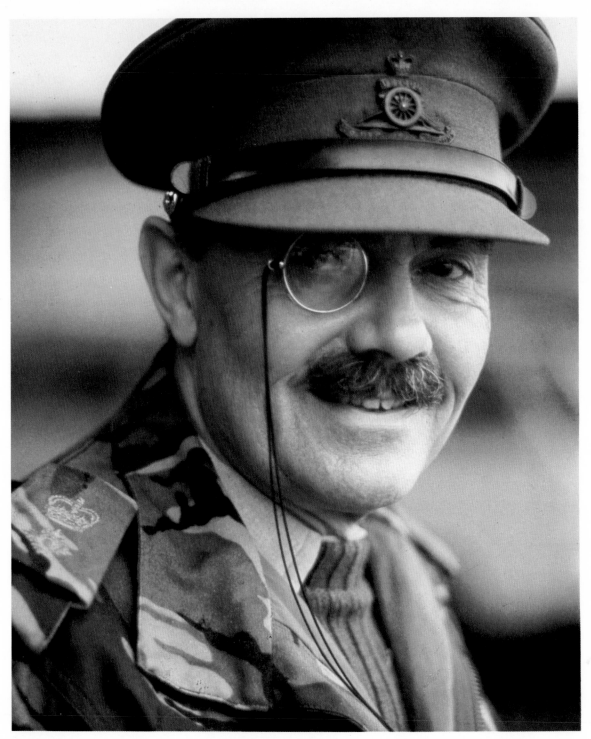

UNITED KINGDOM

The front line of the Royal Air Force consists of over two hundred Tornados and over one hundred F-4 Phantoms. These are supplemented by about fifty VTOL Harriers in the attack role. Roughly three hundred other attack aircraft are equally divided between Jaguar fast attack bombers and Hawk light attack/trainer aircraft. Older types still in service include Buccaneers, Lightwings and Canberras, which add up to a total of about one hundred.

The Royal Naval Air Service has about fifty Sea Harriers which are based on four small aircraft carriers.

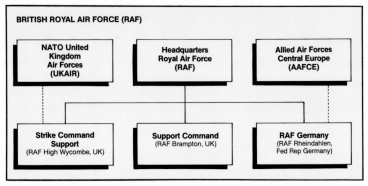

BRITISH ROYAL AIR FORCE (RAF)

NATO United Kingdom Air Forces (UKAIR)	Headquarters Royal Air Force (RAF)	Allied Air Forces Central Europe (AAFCE)
Strike Command Support (RAF High Wycombe, UK)	Support Command (RAF Brampton, UK)	RAF Germany (RAF Rheindahlen, Fed Rep Germany)

Opposite left: British Colonel Guy Long is redolent of the days when there was chivalry in 'the service,' and any self-respecting lad would don his scarf, climb into his Sopwith Camel and do loops over his sweetheart's place in Sussex before heading off to fight 'Jerry.'

In the 1960s, British pilots were more likely to jockey planes along the lines of a British Aerospace Buccaneer *(at left)*, which established itself as a fine attack bomber.

Today's RAF fighter pilot may find himself lucky enough to fly the devastatingly good Panavia Tornado, shown *above* with its Sidewinders (near wing tanks) and belly-mounted Skyflash missiles, during tactical exercises.

Assigned to the RAF Germany, this Harrier 'Jump Jet' (*opposite*) can take off from any level patch of ground, as it is about to do shortly from this 'hide' in the arboreal German countryside—provided the ground crew member at the right of this photograph stops playing with his screwdriver and gets to work!

The Harrier's vectorable-thrust jets make it the only truly successful vertical/short takeoff and landing (VSTOL), reconnaissance/strike aircraft in the world today.

At left: The Harrier 'jumps' into the air. It's not really fast, but it *is* a very good, maneuverable ground strike plane.

Above: A British flight sergeant observes a medical evacuation exercise—bringing 'wounded' from Germany to Great Britain during Reforger 1986.

Above: British airmen converse through the window of an RAF lorry.

Banking left over the European countryside, a British Aerospace Hawk (*at right*) shows its 'talons,' which in this case consist of two AIM-9L Sidewinder Air-to-Air missiles and a centermounted pod containing a 30mm Aden gun and 130 rounds of ammo. The Hawk was designed to be a comprehensive advanced jet trainer for the RAF, but as pictured here, can also be equipped for the emergency intercept role.

Opposite: Royal Navy airpower. In the foreground, an old standby Hawker Hunter, which is being phased out of front line service, flies companion to a brace of 'upstart' Sea Harriers. The Sea Harrier 'jump jet' was designed to be a VSTOL fighter/recon/strike aircraft, and proved itself to be excellent in these capabilities, when Sea Harriers operating from the Royal Navy's aircraft HMS *Invincible* and HMS *Hermes* played a critical role in the British victory of the Falkland Islands conflict in 1982.

Developed from the landbased Harrier GR3, the Sea Harrier differs greatly from the GR3 in its avionics, but the two planes' airframe, power plant and mechanical systems are nearly identical. Standard armament provisions for this aircraft consist of two 30mm Aden guns, and five hardpoint ventral mounts for a wide variety of missiles and bombs.

FRANCE

The French air force is built around a solid centerpiece of over three hundred aircraft from the Dassault-Breguet Mirage series, including more than sixty of the new delta-winged Mirage 2000. Others include over one hundred each Jaguars and Alpha Jets, although the latter are used only for training.

The French Navy, with two full-sized *Clemenceau* class aircraft carriers has a fleet of over one hundred combat aircraft, of which most are Dassault-Breguet Etendards and Super Etendards.

Opposite left: A delta-winged Armee de l'Air Mirage 2000 takes a long drink during a refuelling operation over the Atlantic. This photo was taken from the refueling tanker, an Armee de l'Air C-135.

Center photo, this spread: Here Armee de l'Air Mirage 2000s expend some spunk in the form of pre-takeoff heat waves (note distortion of aircraft in rear). With a 'clean' speed of 1550mph, and a maximum load speed of 690mph, and an operational ceiling of 59,000 feet, the Mirage 2000 is a very capable interceptor and air superiority fighter, with air to ground capability 'coming soon.'

Above left: Mirage 2000s are a popular French export, as is evidenced by this Indian AF Mirage, which both is and is not, strictly speaking, 'maya.'

At immediate left: Reaching for the heights—the Mirage 2000's maximum climb rate is 49,000 feet per minute, and at Mach 2, in an other-than-vertical mode, takes 4 minutes to get to 49,000 feet. The big gray missile visible under this bird's belly is an Exocet anti-ship missile of the type which Argentinian forces used to sink the British destroyer HMS *Sheffield* and the supply ship *Atlantic Conveyor* in the Falkland Islands conflict of 1982.

BELGIUM

Belgium's air force is composed of nearly 20,000 personnel and nearly two hundred combat aircraft, of which over half are F-16 Falcons. The balance are French-built Mirages.

LUXEMBOURG

The smallest country in NATO has no air force of its own, but the 18 Boeing E-3A Sentry Airborne Warning & Control (AWACS) aircraft that are owned by NATO are officially registered in Luxembourg. These aircraft are operated by NATO international crews.

THE NETHERLANDS

The Royal Netherlands Air Force has almost 20,000 personnel and well over two hundred combat aircraft, of which most are F-16s. The others are all F-5s, as the Netherlands' Starfighters have been retired.

Opposite left: A Belgian officer. His Air Force is relatively large for the size of his country, and its equipment, such as the new F-16s, is very good.

Lieutenant Colonel Aria Stobbe (*extreme lower left*) of the Netherlands' Army often works hand in hand with his country's fine F-16-equipped air force.

The US Army in Belgium bolsters that country's forces, and mutual military co-operation is enjoyed, as is witnessed to by this photo of an impromptu conference (*at immediate left*) during a joint US/Belgian airlift operation. Note the Hercules transport in the background.

A Netherlands crew chief (*above*) marshals an F-16 into its parking slot.

CANADA

Officially the Air Command of the unified Armed Forces, Canada's air force has over 20,000 personnel and nearly two hundred combat aircraft. Most of these are divided between F-5s (Canadian designation CF-116), CF-104 Starfighters and CF-18 Hornets, although the CF-104 units are in the process of converting to CF-18s. Canada maintains three squadrons of its CF-18s in Europe as part of its contribution to NATO.

Security is crucial to NATO defense— *above,* a guard checks the ID of a Canadian airman at the entrance to a NATO base.

Right: A Canadian Armed Forces C-130 Hercules awaits a bellyful of troops during a tactical airlift exercise.

The venerable, but tricky, CF-104 Starfighter (*above right*) still figures in Canadian air defense, but is gradually being replaced by the more versatile, and newer, CF-18 Hornet.

A couple of two-seater Hornet trainers (*opposite*) wearing Canada's maple leaf in low-visibility grey bank right over northern lands. The Hornet is a versatile, fast (1350mph 'tops'), multi-role fighter which was originally designed for carrier-based operations.

Norwegian Lieutenant Colonel Fossum (*at right*) has no doubt just 'tasted the air' in one of his country's Mach 2.05 F-16 Falcons.

Below right: A Danish patrol confers while on duty protecting their menagerie of Falcons and Drakens. The Swedish-built F-35 Draken has similar middle-range fighter/ground attack capabilities to the F-16.

Opposite—left to right: US Staff Sergeant Richard Garvey discusses a chemical warfare detection kit with Norwegians Captain T Onarheim and Captain Jahn Hetlelio.

DENMARK

The Danish air force has fewer than 10,000 personnel and just over one hundred combat aircraft. Well over half of these are F-16 Falcons, with the balance being made up of F-104s and Swedish-built F-35 Drakens.

NORWAY

NATO's northernmost air force has fewer than 10,000 personnel and fewer than one hundred combat aircraft, of which most are F-16s and the balance F-5s.

Above: A Spanish naval air arm Harrier II takes to the high canopy of hazy sky.

An Italian guard (*at right*) presents a wary visage on the perimeter of an air base.

A Portuguese A-7 Corsair II (*below opposite*) overflies the Mediterranean. The Corsair II is capable of carrying more than 15,000 pounds of stores under its wings and fuselage, which makes it very useful as an attack bomber.

A swarm of drop tank-equipped Spanish F/A-18 Hornets (*above opposite*) cuts the thin cloud layer above a Southern European landscape; and moments later (*overleaf*) gains altitude—the jock in plane 151-03 hopes that 151-02 is just flashing his navigation light (see tailfin), and not signaling for a left turn, or between 151-02, 03 and 01, it'll be worse than a Barcelona traffic jam.

ITALY

Of Italy's more than three hundred combat aircraft, half are F-104 Starfighters, with the balance being divided between Tornados and G-91 light attack bombers.

PORTUGAL

The Portuguese air arm has just over 10,000 personnel and slightly more than one hundred combat aircraft. These are roughly equally divided between A-7 Corsairs and G-91s, both attack bombers rather than fighters.

SPAIN

NATO's newest member has an air force of over 20,000 with nearly two hundred combat aircraft. Roughly half of these are French-built Mirages, but a growing number are F/A-18 Hornets. There are also about thirty each F-5s and F-4 Phantoms. The Spanish naval air arm also has ten AV-8 Harriers (Spanish designation 'Matador') based on a former US Navy *Independence* class aircraft carrier.

GREECE

The Greek air force has more than 20,000 personnel and over three hundred combat aircraft. Nearly one hundred of these are F-104s, with roughly fifty each of F-4 Phantoms, F-5s and A-7 Crusader attack bombers. Other types include old RF-84s and a growing number of F-16s.

TURKEY

At the southeast corner of NATO's front line, Turkey has the sixth largest air force in the Alliance, with over 50,000 personnel and nearly four hundred combat aircraft. Eventually, almost half this number will be F-16s, but at the present time there are also over one hundred Starfighters, nearly one hundred F-5s, about seventy F-4 Phantoms, and an equal number of aging F-100 Super Sabres, which will be phased out as the F-16s are phased in.

The A-7 Corsair served honorably with the US Navy for many years, and has gained a sturdy reputation as an attack bomber for nations around the world. In this role, it assumes the name of A-7 Crusader, and is shown *above* in service with the Hellenic (Greek) Air Force.

Suitably presented here by an artist, Greek F-16 Hornets (*at right*) overfly the renowned Acropolis, creating a juxtaposition of ancient and modern realities— the Classical Athenian city-state defense system; and the whole of modern Greece as a member of the NATO 'city-state.'

Another General Dynamics artist's conception shows a Turkish F-16 (*opposite*) above present-day Istanbul. This photo is symbolic of what can happen when a defense system fails. The huge domed building below the Falcon was, 1000 years ago, the Byzantine church called Hagia Sophia; was ransacked by turncoat crusaders; and was made into a mosque when the Turks moved in on the fallen city. Istanbul itself was once known as 'Constantinople' after the Roman Emperor Constantine who set up shop there.

CHAPTER 7

Standardization of Equipment Within NATO

Secretary of Defense Caspar Weinberger

Adapted from a Report to the United States Congress by the Secretary of Defense, 31 March 1986

Opposite: F-16 maintenance at Hill Air Force Base, Utah. The 388th Tactical Fighter Wing there was the first fighter wing to fly the F-16, in 1979. As of June 1985, there were more than 1370 F-16s flying for air forces throughout the world.

Standardization within NATO is achieved through several means. Agreement on standard procedures or standard specifications is a fundamental method. Further, we can buy or co-produce one another's equipment, thereby also conserving resources by reducing the duplication of research and development. Finally, we can rationalize NATO's industrial base through armaments cooperation, achieving standardization at the same time as we make the most efficient use of NATO's collective resources.

Over the years we have made substantial progress in standardizing NATO procedures and in standardizing such vital elements as fuels and munitions. Also, defense trade barriers have been broken down to some degree, permitting additional standardization. Co-production arrangements have significantly advanced standardization in selected areas. Notwithstanding these achievements, our progress has been modest and much remains to be done. It is our recognition of this need—and of the need to obtain more conventional defense for our collective investment—which has led in the past year to an increased emphasis on international cooperation in the development of standard weapon systems.

Our emphasis will be on command, control, communication and intelligence projects and on a number of weapon development projects of strong interest to various NATO nations. A

A USAF Staff Sergeant is shown *above* doing some fine tuning on the propellor and air intake of a turboprop aircraft.

***Opposite:* This RAF Tornado carries seven Alarm missiles and two external fuel tanks, as well as, on the outer wings, electronics countermeasures devices in their pods.**

the United Kingdom jointly to embark upon a project for a European Fighter Aircraft (EFA) for the 1990s.

In October 1985, I invited the EFA consortium countries to discuss with the US how we might effectively cooperate with them on this important tactical fighter aircraft program. My hope is that our discussions will lead to a maximum of commonality and interoperability of subsystems and components between their aircraft and our future fighter aircraft development, in order to avoid duplication and to achieve a balanced mix of aircraft on both sides of the Atlantic. We have had an initial round of discussions and have agreed to follow up with meetings by technical experts.

A TEAM EFFORT

Both sides of the Atlantic have agreed that improvements in NATO's conventional posture are required and that progress in NATO armaments cooperation will contribute to that objective. To achieve real progress toward standardization and interoperability within NATO, US leadership is imperative. That leadership must be both farsighted and consistent and must be backed by a broad-based consensus both within and among the Executive Branch, Congress and US industry. This consensus is essential to the development of programs to implement our national policy of armaments cooperation.

THE ROLE OF USCINCEUR

In his theater of operations, the US Commander in Chief Europe (USCINCEUR) employs the full range of sea, land and air assets. The deficiencies identified in the 1985 report generally remain, due in part to lengthy acquisition lead times. Additionally, differing national views on equipment development requirements and limitations continue to delay attainment of NATO's interoperability goals. One of NATO's most critical operational problems, now and in the foreseeable future, is the integration of NATO Air Defense Forces, both ground and air elements. The fact that NATO has to resort to an indirect identification process, that depends solely on demanding air space control procedures, results in cumbersome, nonresponsive procedures and weapon identification zones, and restrictions on Beyond-Visual-Range (BVR) capabilities that diminish a major advantage potentially held over Warsaw Pact air forces. The critical link to the entire air defense structure is the NATO Identification System (NIS) which would al-

large factor in the selection of cooperative project candidates will be a project's applicability to the correction of critical deficiencies in conventional military capabilities noted by NATO Defense Ministers. The intent is to identify discrete programs which will help redress critical deficiencies in NATO conventional forces and then give these programs priority within the nations. We will maximize our support through adequate funding of those programs and through sharing of technology as an inducement to, and commensurate with, the commitment of the Allies.

The Independent European Program Group (IEPG) has continued its efforts to provide high-level political support to strengthen the contribution of the European member nations to Alliance arms collaboration. Member nations have agreed on initial steps aimed at harmonizing national equipment requirements and timetables for procurement; have launched the first of a series of Cooperative Technology Projects (CTP); and have begun work on a major study of ways of improving the competitiveness of European defense industry. Also, several new collaborative ventures at the project level have been started, notably the agreement of Germany, Italy, Spain and low friendly aircraft greater freedom to operate over the battlefield.

Recently, the US and several NATO nations (France, Germany and the UK) agreed to a baseline for an improved NIS system that provides anti-jam capability in a hostile environment. However, tactical command and control systems continue to suffer from separate national development in areas such as tactical switching systems and tactical radios, resulting in the inability to net these systems. This problem becomes particularly crucial when NATO commanders are attempting to maintain combat coordination at the interface of corps operations involving differing nations. The basic portion of NATO Standardization Agreement (STANAG) 4175 (Multi-functional Information Distribution System (MIDS)) has recently been agreed upon by all nations. It is expected that the MIDS STANAG will be sent to nations for formal ratification during 1986. It is also expected that the Military Operational Requirement for MIDS in NATO will be approved in 1986. However, there continues to be delay in commitment to LINK-16 for use with the Joint Tactical Information Distribution System (JTIDS) on the NATO AWACS, air defense ground sites and MIDS. A common data link language (LINK-16/TADIL-J) is required if US JTIDS and the proposed STANAG 4175 MIDS are to be implemented in NATO. The US JTIDS/TADIL-J effort will provide secure digital data exchange between aircraft, ground command and control centers and ships, and has the potential to effect a secure voice capability between US forces and the NATO defense systems, but only if NATO will commit to both LINK-16 and MIDS. NATO has previously ratified the HAVE QUICK STANAG, and several nations are planning to modify existing systems with HAVE QUICK/ HAVE QUICK II capabilities, thereby yielding a significant anti-jam voice capability for the NATO tactical air forces.

NATO AIR DEFENSE COMMITTEE

In November 1980 a NATO Air Defense Committee (NADC) was established to harmonize military requirements and risks associated with air defense, as stated by the NATO Military Authorities, with pertinent political, economic, industrial and technological factors obtained from nations and other NATO bodies. Concerned with short-term problems as well as long-term plans, this committee is NATO's senior body on air defense matters. Through three subordinate panels it has investigated a number of complex areas including the up-

The British Rapier ultra low-level air defense system (*below*) is designed to destroy attack aircraft flying under most existing radar 'nets.' In this photo of a Rapier test firing, note the Rapier system's multi-directional 'turret' launch platform and the sensing equipment at its extreme left.

The Night Chaparral short range air defense system—shown in action *opposite* during a test firing—could operate in Central Europe for 85 percent of all weather contingencies—an important consideration, given the climate in that area. Night Chaparral is an extension of the US Army's Chaparral short-range air defense system, which consists of four SAMs mounted on a multi-directional, mobile launch platform.

dating of the NATO 1979 air defense program, designing an integrated command and control system for all air operations, and studying ways of integrating the effects of offensive counter-air with established air defense operations.

A group of experts under the NATO Air Defense Committee has completed updating the NATO Air Defense Program approved by Defense Ministers in 1979, taking into account new considerations and revisions in national resources and commitments. This interim report is undergoing analytical validation. At the same time SACEUR has completed a comprehensive review of NATO's air defense capability, the results of which must be harmonized with efforts to update the air defense program and then presented to Defense Ministers for approval as NATO's new road map toward an improved integrated air defense posture.

The SACEUR study on how best to fight and win the 'air defense battle' in Europe was conducted by the SHAPE Air Defense Ad Hoc Working Group. The final report of the Working Group, culminating a 14-month study effort, was forwarded to the NATO Military Committee (MC) in September 1984 for endorsement. The MC is staffing the report in-

crementally through its Air Defense Study Working Group, with national inputs and assistance from SACEUR's newly-formed Air Planning Team.

Significant improvements have been made in NATO's air defense coverage through initiatives on providing point defense at our air bases in Europe. As previously noted, a cooperative agreement was signed with the United Kingdom for acquisition of the Rapier air defense system, an agreement which has become a 'role model' for other programs. Innovative agreements have been signed with Germany for its acquisition of the Patriot air defense system. The Netherlands and the US have entered into a separate arrangement for The Netherlands' Patriot. An agreement has been reached with Turkey for acquisition of Rapier, which is an extension of the US/UK Rapier Agreement. A Letter of Intent (LOI) has been signed with the UK for the Rapier purchase. Agreements with Belgium are being pursued, and talks with Italy are under way. These agreements will result in enhanced effectiveness and interoperability in the air defense of NATO.

Integrated command and control of all air operations is central to effective conduct of Alliance air defense. A team of

over 30 technical experts from NATO member countries was formed during 1982 to develop the design for the improvement and integration of NATO's air command and control system (ACCS). US participation includes leadership of two of the five major functional divisions. This effort is an important command and control initiative that NATO has undertaken because ACCS can provide a framework to integrate many major strategic and tactical command and control, communications and intelligence systems of the future. The ACCS improvements will include infrastructure, multinational and national funded capabilities in its architecture.

Progress has been made toward defining and refining military requirements as well as the baseline capabilities from which this modernization program will evolve. In September 1983 SHAPE published an ACCS Military Operational Requirements (MOR) document which outlines the requirements for modernization. Regional supplements to the ACCS MOR were published in May 1984. The ACCS Team has recently drafted three documents which further refine C^3 requirements: ACCS Goals, Baseline Capabilities, and ACCS Needs. The ACCS team is subordinate to the NADC's Panel on the Airspace Management and Control System, which is planning the evolution of the team into a full-fledged NATO management agency.

The SACEUR Air Defense Ad Hoc Working Group has confirmed the need for a mix of densely packed Surface to Air Missile Systems (SAMs), Short Range Air Defenses (SHORADs) and fighters. It also identified weaknesses in current Medium Surface to Air Missile Systems (MSAM). The Panel on Air Defense Weapons, in accordance with guidance provided by the NATO Air Defense Committee, identified two approaches to resolve these MSAM deficiencies—gradually improve HAWK or develop a new system. The Committee of National Armaments Directors (CNAD) was tasked to accomplish the MSAM analysis, and Air Group VI was established as a subgroup of the NATO Air Forces Armaments Group to do the work. Air Group VI developed an Outline NATO Staff Target (ONST) that lists characteristics of a proposed MSAM. The US and other nations are staffing this ONST and will participate in the system development through Air Group VI, other NATO Air Defense panels/committees and other bilateral agreements with NATO nations. This MSAM effort is one of our prime candidates for cooperative development.

Critical to the interoperability of command and control systems is the exchange of data in a useable fashion. For auto-

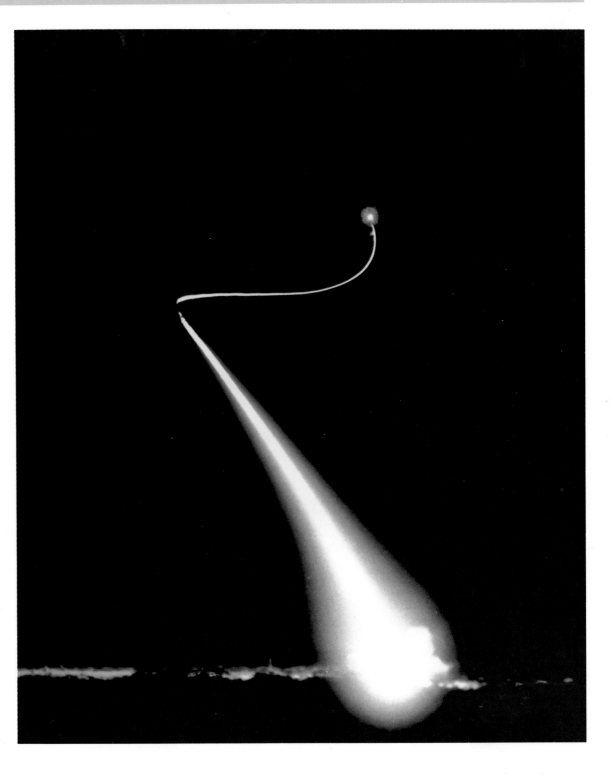

Above: Two jet engine mechanics—one from the Canadian Armed Forces (in sweater), and one from the US Air Force—examine an intake duct of one of the four Pratt & Whitney TF33 turbofan engines which are the power that lifts the Boeing E-3A AWACS (*opposite,* with radome) into the air.

Delivering 21,000 pounds of thrust each, the TF33s boost the fully loaded 325,000-pound aircraft to its mission parameters of 21,000 feet at a range of 11,550 miles from base for a seven-hour shift. The plane's unrefueled endurance time is 11.5 hours.

The AWACS' main identifying feature is the characteristic 'skunk-striped' 30-foot diameter radar dome which rotates at 6 rpm while in operation, and incorporates the AN/APY-1 surveillance radar and IFF TADIL antennae. The plane's initial Westinghouse radar is of the pulse-Doppler variety, which provides long range accuracy and look-down capability.

The heart of the AWACS is an IBM 4-Pi CC-1 high speed computer. The E-3A's communications equipment includes High Frequency, VHF and UHF for transmission/reception of information in both code and uncoded forms—and is both vocal and digital in mode.

The AWACS functions as a surveillance and battle control station. In the foreground of the photo *at opposite* is an F-16 Fighting Falcon, one of the types of aircraft AWACS would control if war broke out.

mated data handling, the form and content of the data to be exchanged must be standardized. The development and management of the NATO standardization agreements in this area are accomplished by the Allied Data Systems Interoperability Agency (ADSIA). Through this agency, the United States has introduced the tactical data link TADIL-A into NATO as LINK 11 for use by allied navies as well as the NATO AEW&C System. This group, with US continued participation in it, will assure standardization between US TADIL-J (to be used by JTIDS) and NATO LINK 16 (to be used by the NATO equivalent systems). The US supports the ADSIA with delegations, working group chairmen and significant staff support.

As a result of US initiatives, NATO is closely examining its overall counter-air (offensive and defensive) capability. SACEUR's Air Planning Team and the NADC's Panels on Air Defense Philosophy and Air Defense Weapons are both working to provide the insight necessary to determine the weapon systems required to counter the growing Pact threat and examining how to integrate offensive counter-air considerations into NATO air defense concepts. Great challenges lie ahead in the harmonization of military requirements for both air defense and offensive counter-air with factors such as affordability, exploitable technology and support for cooperative development.

NATO AIRBORNE EARLY WARNING (AEW) SYSTEM

Through the contributions and participation of 13 of the 16 NATO nations, the NATO Airborne Early Warning and Control (AEW&C) Force has become a reality. This multibillion dollar effort includes the joint purchase and ownership of 18 Boeing E-3A Sentry aircraft, the upgrade of ground radar sites throughout Europe and activation of a Main Operating Base, three Forward Operating Bases (in Greece, Turkey and Italy) and a Forward Operating Location in Norway. The aircraft are being manned and supported by over 2400 personnel from all of the participating nations. This force is being integrated into the overall NATO air defense program. This cooperative project represents the first major NATO full time operational force in the history of NATO and provides an AEW capability throughout NATO's area of interest. As of April 1985 all E-3As have been delivered and the NATO E-3A component attained Initial Operational Capability (IOC). The arrangement benefits the US in that over 60 percent of the investment is

138

The General Dynamics F-16 Falcon

The military insignias of the F-16 Fighting Falcon user nations (*left to right, top row, then bottom row):* Belgium (NATO), Denmark (NATO), Egypt, Greece (NATO), Israel, South Korea, The Netherlands (NATO), Norway (NATO), Pakistan, Turkey (NATO), Singapore, the USA (NATO) and Venezuela.

The F-16A Falcon *at below right* looks a bit like a shark, and it is indeed representative of a breed of furious fighters, capable of Mach 2 at 60,000 feet and armed with one General Electric M61 20mm cannon, plus the capability of platforming a wide variety of lethal stores including AIM Sidewinder missiles, the Paveway I 'smart bomb,' the entire line of AGM Maverick ASMs, and many other air-to-air, air-to-ground and electronic guidance and warfare systems.

At 32 feet, 10 inches across the wings by 49 feet, four inches 'by the beam,' the Falcon is a handy bird, a 'good turner' as well as being fast, though its high speed avionics prohibit any low speed dogfighting—'slam-bam' is its style and it does it well.

The illustration *at middle right* shows the basic Falcon silhouettes. The F-16D is the trainer version of the F-16C, just as the F-16B is the trainer version of the F-16A.

Extreme opposite: Two Hill AFB F-16As cut clean profiles against the sky.

NAVSTAR, the US-developed NATO Global Positioning System satellite (*above*), will greatly enhance navigational control for NATO forces—sort of a 'super AWACS.'

made by other participants, and this reduces the burden of US AEW requirements in Europe.

The opportunity also exists to establish joint US/NATO arrangements for common modifications to both US and NATO E-3As in those instances where our requirements are common.

US AIR FORCE PROGRAMS SUPPORTING COMMON NATO REQUIREMENTS

Advanced Medium-Range Air-to-Air Missile (AMRAAM). AMRAAM is an all-weather, all-aspect missile with an active radar seeker. This missile will provide the capability for multiple launches at multiple targets at medium range. It becomes autonomous soon after launch to permit the launch aircraft to maneuver and/or engage more targets quickly. AMRAAM will be compatible with the F-14, F-15, F-16 and F/A-18 aircraft, as well as the German F-4F and the UK Sea Harrier and Tornado aircraft. Full-scale development began in 1981, with the first production delivery in 1988 to the US Air Force. US Navy deliveries are scheduled for 1991.

In August 1980 the US signed an agreement with France, Germany and the UK for a cooperative program for a family of air-to-air missile systems. Germany, the UK and the US are full participants while France is a signatory government only. The agreement provides for the US to develop AMRAAM for use by all participants to satisfy the medium range missile requirement defined in the 'Operational Objective for NATO Air-to-Air Missiles for the 1980s and Beyond.' In accordance with the agreement, the Europeans may choose to buy AMRAAM through foreign military sales, to coassemble AMRAAM or to dual-produce AMRAAM. Canada and Italy are observer governments under the agreement. Additionally, as provided in the agreement, Germany and the UK will develop the Advanced Short Range Air-to-Air Missile (ASRAAM). Norway has joined with them in the ASRAAM Program.

Joint Tactical Information Distribution System (JTIDS) Class I Terminal. JTIDS Class I terminal is a highly jam-resistant, secure, digital information distribution system for use in a tactical combat environment. In 1976 the US formally proposed that NATO adopt JTIDS Class I terminal as the basis for jam-resistant communications throughout the Alliance. In December 1978 JTIDS Class I terminal was adopted as the ECM-Resistant Communications System (ERCS) for the

NATO Airborne Early Warning and Control (AEW&C) Program. Production of JTIDS Class I terminal for this NATO program began in July 1980, with the first delivery in June 1983. The first production-line E-3A with JTIDS Class I installed was delivered to NATO in November 1983. Meanwhile, air-ground interoperability testing, using JTIDS Class I preproduction terminals in operational aircraft, was completed in early 1983. Germany is coproducing JTIDS Class I terminals for all the NATO ground sites and the last 10 of 18 NATO E-3 aircraft and has participated (both with the UK and alone) in equipment compatibility tests to help achieve frequency clearance for JTIDS.

European national clearances for JTIDS operations by the NATO Airborne Early Warning and Control (AEW&C) force started to be issued in December 1982, with Germany first. The UK has selected JTIDS Class 2 terminals for its Tornado interceptors, its Nimrod AEW aircraft and four of its ground radar sites. Having completed its JTIDS evaluation under an October 1978 agreement, the UK will procure these terminals under a September 1983 JTIDS agreement. France signed an agreement in February 1980 to make its SINTAC System interoperable with JTIDS and is continuing a national development program. The NATO Multifunctional Information Distribution System (MIDS) Project Group is completing its work on a NATO Standardization Agreement for MIDS based upon the US JTIDS Class 2 TDMA Specification and, if NATO interest will support it, may initiate a NATO MIDS project.

HAVE QUICK/HAVE QUICK II. The US-developed HAVE QUICK anti-jam voice communication system provides a near-term capability for tactical voice communications. The HAVE QUICK II program is developing improvements to the HAVE QUICK system which will enhance its jam-resistance and ease its operational usage. HAVE QUICK II is the first US ECM-resistant communication system to obtain NATO frequency support. It should provide a significant tactical voice capability into the 1990s.

NAVSTAR Global Positioning System. The NAVSTAR Global Positioning System (GPS) is a space-based radio navigation system which will provide significant improvement over current radio navigation systems in coverage, accuracy, survivability and availability. GPS will also provide a common positioning grid for air, land and sea forces, including reconnaissance elements. Installation of GPS receivers in US military aircraft, ships, tanks, missiles, trucks and jeeps will start in 1987.

The NATO GPS Project, a cooperative venture among the US and nine other NATO nations, was established in April 1978. NATO GPS project activities have included flight tests on aircraft of NATO allies, an ECM Vulnerability Study, ship and submarine trials and development and approval of a NATO standard interface control document. In 1983 a revised agreement was negotiated for continuing the cooperative development effort. It also contained the US commitment on the availability of GPS to NATO in both peacetime and wartime. Engineers from the participating NATO nations are assigned to the GPS Program Office where they are supporting the development program. NATO GPS activities are funded entirely by the NATO participants other than the US.

AGM-65 Maverick. The Maverick missile is a self-guided, rocket-propelled air-to-surface missile designed to destroy small, hard tactical targets in the close-air support, interdiction, defense suppression and counter-air operations of tactical air forces. The development of this missile began in 1968 and has resulted in a 'family' of terminal guidance seekers mated to a common center/aft section. The television (TV) version provides a daylight launch-and-leave capability. Production missiles delivered include the AGM-65A (TV) and the AGM-65B (TV-scene magnification) Maverick. Full-Scale Engineering Development of the AGM-65D Imaging Infrared (IR) Maverick was initiated in October 1978. A DSARC III was held in March 1982. US production of IR Maverick started in September 1982 with the first AGM-65D delivered in October 1983. This version will provide a day/night under-adverse-weather weapon system while retaining the launch-and-leave capability of the basic TV Maverick. The AGM-65G uses the imaging infrared seeker with a 300 pound blast/fragmentation warhead for use against hardened targets. Several allied countries, including Germany, Greece and Turkey, have purchased TV Maverick (AGM-65A/B) through US Foreign Military Sales procedures. We have signed a Memorandum of Understanding (MOU) for NATO coproduction of AGM-65D with Italy leading a NATO consortium, which also includes Germany, the Netherlands, Denmark and Turkey.

The A-10 Thunderbolt, aka 'Warthog', (*above*) carries a Maverick AGM-65A missile (the white missile under the A-10's wing), which is a television-guided ground attack missile with launch-and-leave capability, meaning that it finds its own way to the target. The Maverick was first used in 1972 in Vietnam and still equips all of TAC's first-line fighter bombers and attack aircraft.

The Fairchild Republic A-10 Thunderbolt II

Below: This cutaway view of the A-10 Thunderbolt shows, from front to rear, instrument landing system (ILS), GAU-8/A Avenger 30mm gun, cockpit, selective interrogation and interrogation friend or foe electronics, General Electric TF34-100 turbofans, and rear stabilizer.

The USAF insignia (*above right*). USAF is the only service that uses the A-10.

Seen at right virtually soaring on its large wing area, the 'Warthog' is an unparalleled ground attack devastator, capable of loading its base operating weight of 24,918 pounds up to 50,000 pounds with munitions.

Opposite, above: The Warthog at rest.

Opposite, below: A full-scale mockup of the Hog's GAU-8 30mm cannon seems to dwarf the Volkwagen parked next to it.

US NAVY EXISTING PROGRAMS

T-45 Training System (T-45TS, formerly VTXTS). This program calls for the procurement of 300 T-45A Goshawk training aircraft, 32 simulators and 49 computer-aided devices which will be integrated into a complete training system. The carrier-suitable Goshawk, which is a derivative of the Hawk trainer being produced by British Aerospace (BAe) for the UK Royal Air Force, will replace current US Navy intermediate- and advanced-phase jet training aircraft, which are nearing the end of their service life. On 2 October 1984, the McDonnell Douglas Corporation was awarded a contract for the full-scale engineering development of the T-45 training system. McDonnell Douglas and BAe have agreed to split the airframe production effort. Other UK firms involved include Rolls Royce (turbine fan engines); Plessey (fuel boost pumps and electrical generators); Vickers (hydraulic pumps); Lucas (electrical activators) and Dowdy (ram air turbines, indicators and hydraulic valves). The first 12 aircraft with associated ground equipment are scheduled to be operational by 1990. Total acquisition cost is about $5 billion.

AV-8B Harrier. The AV-8B is an improved version of the UK-developed AV-8A Harrier V/STOL (Vertical/Short Takeoff and Landing) aircraft, which has been operational in the USMC since 1971. The AV-8B has better range/payload performance characteristics than the AV-8A, and its reliability and maintainability are improved. In June 1981 the US and UK governments signed an MOU for the development, production and support of the AV-8B and its UK counterpart, the GR MK 5. McDonnell Douglas, the prime contractor for the US, is responsible for final assembly of 328 AV-8Bs, while the UK prime contractor, British Aerospace, will supply the fuselage for all aircraft as well as assemble approximately 100 GR MK 5s for the RAF. The Rolls Royce Pegasus II engine will be installed in both the AV-8B and the GR MK 5.

ALLIED EQUIPMENT UNDER US EVALUATION

Rapier Air Defense Missile System. The US Air Force is procuring the UK Rapier air defense missile system. The short-range, all-weather Rapier system will satisfy a long-standing Supreme Allied Commander Europe (SACEUR) requirement for air defense for US air bases in the UK. Under the agreement the US is procuring 32 Rapier systems, supporting equipment and logistics support. The UK will provide

Rapier manning, maintenance and training of Royal Air Force personnel in return for a reduction in the Trident missile research and development recoupment costs. An agreement was signed on 13 February 1981 to establish the general terms of this arrangement. Specific terms for operations and support were completed in a separate Operations and Support Annex which was signed in November 1983. A formal letter of Offer and Acceptance was completed in December 1982. The first USAF Rapier Squadron achieved its initial operational capability in November 1984. Also in November 1984 the US and the Government of Turkey signed a broad agreement following the 'Rapier role model' concept using the Rapier missile system for point air defense of US bases in Turkey. Details of the arrangement are nearing completion. The US has agreed to buy and Turkey has agreed to operate and maintain 14 Rapier fire units to defend Incirlik Air Base and Cigli Air Base. This arrangement furthers commonality goals in NATO since the government of Turkey has the Rapier missile system in its inventory. Rapier equipment will be procured by supplement to the existing US-UK Rapier agreement.

EIFEL Program. EIFEL is a German-developed data management and command and control system which automates selected tactical offensive air command and control functions. The present version EIFEL I is being used in the two German-operated Central Region Allied Tactical Operations Centers (ATOCs) and in the US-operated ATOC at Sembach, Germany. By procuring the system, all four ATOCS in the NATO Central Region will have common equipment, since the fourth ATOC is also installing the EIFEL I system. Ultimately the result will be a standardized system based upon the most advanced technology. A joint US/German study completed in January 1982 resulted in a program plan for joint development known as EIFEL Follow-On Program. The EIFEL Follow-On Program will expand/augment the EIFEL I System. An agreement to participate in the cooperative development of EIFEL Follow-On was signed by DoD and German Ministry of Defense representatives in October 1982. The USAF EIFEL Follow-On effort is led by the Air Force Systems Command, Electronic Systems Division—Europe with heavy involvement of US Air Forces Europe.

A joint (US/German) EIFEL Follow-On Program Office has been established and has drafted an MOU for the joint program. The EIFEL Follow-On Program will assure the USAF in Europe of full interoperability with the NATO allies and provide continued enhancement of operational capabilities.

NATO Air Base SATCOM (NABS) Program. The United States concluded in November 1982 a Memorandum of Understanding with NATO on the NABS Program. This program will greatly enhance the survivability of combat-essential communications for our air bases in Europe. It will provide a survivable, jam-resistant and very flexible satellite communications system to ensure wartime communications connectivity for US, NATO and host nation purposes at collocated operating bases, main operating bases and air operations centers. This is a joint US/NATO initiative and additional terminals may be procured by NATO and/or host nations via the Foreign Military Sales Program. As presently defined, USAF will procure approximately 82 terminals to satisfy its requirements (and most of these incidentally support certain critical NATO and host nation requirements), and NATO will provide satellite support.

Wide-angle Head-Up Display (HUD) Unit for the General Dynamics F-16 Fighting Falcon tactical fighter. The US Air

Opposite: A Sea Harrier at altitude with load of M82 Snakeye retarded bombs on its wing pylons. Note the scorching on the plane's underbelly and wings, due to its unique jet exhaust arrangement.

Above: This is a pilot's eye view of the F-16 Fighting Falcon's control panel, complete with Head Up Display, which allows the pilot to read essential instrument data without taking his 'eyes off the road.'

The British Aerospace Harrier/ McDonnell Douglas AV-8 Harrier

Above, right: The military insignia of the Harrier's user nations, *from left to right:* India, Spain, the United Kingdom and the USA. The Marine Corps is the user service in the latter nation. The Harrier originally evolved in Britain from an original Hawker design. Currently, Harriers are produced by British Aerospace and in the United States under license by McDonnell Douglas.

By vectoring its exhaust jets, the Harrier (*at right*) can take off vertically, and land the same way. While capable of conventional landings, it's actually safer to do it vertically. Not only that, the Harrier can vector in flight as well, giving it the capability of nearly stopping still at altitude— which gives the McDonnell Douglas British Aerospace Harrier an unprecedented advantage as a maneuvering fighter; with the right pilot, the Harrier can beat anything now being flown, and Sea Harriers proved this extraordinary maneuverability in the Falkland Islands conflict.

Opposite: Three US Marine Corps AV-8A Harrier IIs participate in an operation near the West German border. Note the Snakeye bombs under their wings.

Extreme opposite: The AV-8's three profiles. *Opposite, below:* This cutaway of a Sea Harrier shows, *from left to right,* laser-ranger and marked-target seeker electronics, target seeker camera, cockpit, avionics system including the Head Up Display and Blue Fox radar electronics, Rolls Royce/Pegasus 105 afterburning turbofan engine (21,750 pounds of thrust), vectorable exhaust nozzles (rotated aft for forward flight), VHF and UHF radio electronics and tail.

Above and opposite: An F/A-18 Hornet comes up to a US Air Force KC-135 Stratotanker for a drink. The Spanish, Canadian and US Navy/Marine Corps F/A-18s can be refuelled by US Air Force tankers using the hose and drogue that's deployed from the boom—as is shown in these photos. Canada, Britain and the US Navy/Marine Corps also maintain aerial refuelling aircraft which use hose and drogue method only. The French C-135F refuelling fleet is equipped with aerial booms, but use the procedure shown here. (See also page 153)

Force is installing Marconi-built (UK) wide-angle conventional head-up display units in its F-16 C/D aircraft. Deliveries began in 1984. Total quantities to be purchased will be approximately 1200, with deliveries running through 1993. In addition, the US Air Force will install Marconi wide-angle raster HUDS in 250 LANTIRN-equipped F-16s. The total cost for these HUDs will be approximately $86.9 million with deliveries in 1989 and 1990.

Flycatcher Radar. The US Air Force accepted delivery of a Flycatcher radar system from the Netherlands in February 1984 for test range support at Eglin Air Force Base, Florida. Purchase price was approximately $3 million. The Air Force will also acquire a series of upgrades and modifications through 1986 at an expected cost of $2 million.

Lightweight Decontamination System (LDS). The LDS is a Norwegian decontamination system which produces hot water or steam to remove chemical agents from objects. It also has a shower capability and the entire system is man-portable. Delivery of 250 units in 1986 completed the USAF buy of 1800 units.

Durandal Airfield Attack Weapon. The French Durandal airfield attack weapon is being procured by the USAF as a result of a successful Foreign Weapons Evaluation Program. The USAF has contracted to buy 3434 Durandals. Deliveries began in February 1984. The USAF plans to acquire approximately 5451 additional units.

US NAVY PROGRAMS FOR PROCUREMENT AND USE BY NATO ALLIES

Sparrow Advanced Monopulse Missile (AMM) AIM/RIM-7M. The Sparrow AIM/RIM-7M is a joint US Navy/Air Force program intended to provide the Services with an improved medium-range, all-weather air-to-air missile and an improved surface-to-air missile for the NATO SeaSparrow System. The RIM-7M, a surface-to-air version, has been released to all NATO SeaSparrow surface missile system owners.

AIM-9L Infrared Air-to-Air Missile. The AIM-9L Sidewinder is an improved passive infrared-homing, short range air-to-air missile. As a result of a Memorandum of Understanding signed by the US and Germany in 1977, Germany heads a European consortium to coproduce the AIM-9L missile, less the active optical detector. Other members of the consortium are Norway, the UK and Italy. The AIM-9L is employed on the F-4, F-14, AV-8, F-16, F-15, A-6, A-7, AH-1T, F/A-18 and the Tornado. This Sidewinder missile differs from its predecessors principally in its versatile all-aspect attack capability.

High-Speed Antiradiation Missile (HARM). HARM is designed to destroy or suppress land and sea-based radars involved with enemy air defense systems. The joint US Air Force/Navy missile system is a design evolution with greatly increased capabilities over current antiradiation missiles. Initial production of HARM started in 1981. HARM provides a greatly expanded, destructive, defense-suppression capability. Its high-speed, long-range and broad-frequency coverage in a single seeker provides a significant improvement over Shrike and Standard ARM. HARM has been approved for Foreign Military Sales to NATO nations. Coproduction will be approved on a case-by-case basis for noncritical technology components. The US offered HARM to NATO in 1979 as one of 17 dual-production candidates.

F/A-18 Naval Strike Fighter Aircraft. The F/A-18 Naval Strike Fighter will replace the F-4 and A-7 in Navy/Marine fighter and attack squadrons. The F/A-18 will be mission-convertible to accomplish fighter or attack missions. Canada selected the F/A-18 (CF-18) as its new combat fighter and is purchasing 138 aircraft over a six-year period 1982-87. A commercial contract between the Canadian Government and McDonnell Douglas was signed in 1980 and there is considerable participation by other Canadian firms in the project. US Government support is outlined in a government-to-government agreement signed in November 1981. Spain will purchase 72 F/A-18s (EF-18) with an option to purchase 12 more.

P-3 Patrol Aircraft. The US Navy P-3 Orion is a maritime patrol aircraft with the primary mission of antisubmarine warfare (ASW). It is one of NATO's most effective and economical ASW systems and is presently operated by the navies of the US, Norway, The Netherlands, Portugal, Spain and Canada (as the Aurora). Germany, Greece and Turkey have expressed interest in the P-3. Spain has expressed an interest in upgrading its P-3s, and Norway intends to replace some of its P-3Bs with new P-3C aircraft.

E-2C Early Warning Aircraft. The twin turboprop Hawkeye is a carrier- and land-based early warning aircraft. It is capable of transmitting contact data via voice or data link to control centers or interceptor aircraft. This aircraft was briefed to France and Greece in FY 83, to Turkey in FY 84 and to Spain in FY 85.

McDonnell Douglas F/A-18 Hornet

Above right, from left to right: The military insignia of the F/A-18 Hornet are Australia, Canada, Spain and the USA.

At right: This underbelly view of a US Navy F/A-18 Hornet reveals that this plane is tricked out for a reconnaissance mission—which is evidenced by the camera ports near the plane's nose. The AIM-9L Sidewinders on its wingtips are blue—signifying that they are 'window dressing'—aka inert dummies. The Canadian CF-18 Hornet *at above opposite,* however, wears a real Sidewinder AAM on its visible wingtip, while underwing is an AIM-7 Sparrow medium-range AAM.

The Hornet has a 40-foot eight inch wingspan, is 56 feet long, and weighs 33,580 pounds. Its standard armament includes a brace of fuselage-mounted AIM-7 Sparrow missiles, two wingtip-mounted AIM-9 Sidewinders and one General Electric M61 20mm multibarrelled cannon.

Below opposite: These two F/A-18 Hornets of fighter-attack squadron (VFA) 25 are positioned on the takeoff catapults of the aircraft carrier USS *Constellation.*

Extreme opposite: Three views of an F/A-18.

*Canada uses the designation CF-18 for its Hornets.

Above: A SAC airman concentrates on operating the controls of the refuelling probe, on board a USAFE KC-135 Stratotanker, during the refuelling of an F-15.

Opposite: A French C-135F Stratotanker at rest on a typically rainy French airfield. Note the refuelling probe boom beneath its tail. The French C-135F is essentially identical to the US Air Force KC-135 series. Both tankers are built by Boeing under the company model designation 717, and not 707 as is often erroneously reported.

US AIR FORCE PROGRAMS FOR PROCUREMENT AND USE BY THE NATO ALLIES

The following USAF programs continue to show potential for procurement and use by NATO allies. Some are already being procured and used by the allies and have been discussed in more detail in preceding sections of this report.

F-16 Multinational Fighter Program. The European Participating Governments (EPG) consortium to produce the F-16 was formed in 1975 by Belgium, Denmark, the Netherlands and Norway. To date the consortium has produced approximately 355 aircraft. Production is expected to continue through 1993 with an expected total of 503 aircraft. Other NATO purchasers of the F-16 include Turkey and Greece. Turkey has contracted for 160 F-16 C/D aircraft with deliveries beginning in 1987 and lasting through 1994. Greece has selected the F-16 C/D for part of its next fighter buy. Negotiations for direct commercial sale of 40 aircraft are currently under way.

NATO Airborne Early Warning and Control (AEW&C) Program. Initially 12 NATO nations signed the MOU establishing the NATO AEW&C Program. Belgium, a nonsignatory to the aircraft component, subsequently agreed to full participation in the program. NATO has procured and taken delivery of 18 aircraft. In addition, 15 modified Air Defense Ground Environment sites were accepted, providing the capability to integrate the E-3A air picture with ground radar data.

NAVSTAR Global Positioning System (GPS). There are 10 NATO nations participating in the NATO GPS Program. Decisions by the participating allies about integrating GPS equipment into their military forces are being made in 1986.

Joint Tactical Information Distribution System (JTIDS). This system was adopted as the jam-resistant communications system for the NATO AEW&C Program. Standardization and interoperability efforts are continuing under the aegis of the NATO Multifunctional Information Distribution System (MIDS) Project Group.

AGM-65 Maverick. Germany has purchased 450 AGM-65B missiles through Foreign Military Sales (FMS). Turkey has purchased 100 AGM-65A missiles, and Greece has purchased 100 AGM-65A and 200 AGM-65B missiles.

Advanced Medium-Range Air-to-Air Missile (AMRAAM). Germany, the UK and the US are participating governments in the Air-to-Air Family of Weapons Missile Systems MOU. France is a signatory government and Norway has requested that it be accepted as a participating government. Canada and Italy are observer governments under the terms of the MOU. Participating governments intend to acquire or dual produce AMRAAM, while observers have expressed interest in acquiring the missiles.

KC-135 Re-engining (CFM-56). The Air Force is modernizing the KC-135A tanker fleet with the CFM-56 engine, jointly produced by General Electric and SNECMA (a French national company). The French Air Force joined the program in order to re-engine its 11 C-135F aircraft concurrently with the USAF program. The French government contributed $28.5 million as a pro rata share of the KC-135R development program and has contracted for the first French C-135F modification under a Foreign Military Sales agreement with the USAF.

Communication Satellites. The last of the NATO III communication satellites was launched in November 1984. NATO was evaluating the British SKYNET IV satellite and the US Defense Satellite Communications System (DSCS) III satellite to provide communications in the 1990s. The US offer has expired and was not renewed. NATO has agreed to fund SKYNET IV through sole source procurement.

CODEVELOPMENT AND/OR COPRODUCTION BY US NAVY WITH ALLIES

Penguin Missile. The Penguin missile is a Norwegian infrared, countermeasures resistant, helicopter launched, offensive antiship weapon. The Penguin program entered full scale engineering development in January 1986 as a result of a contract signed between the Government of Norway and the United States Navy. A production Memorandum of Understanding is under negotiation.

NATO SeaSparrow Point Defense Missile System. The NATO SeaSparrow Surface Missile System (NSSMS) provides ships with an effective short-range, quick-reaction, self-defense capability against a wide spectrum of threats, including low-altitude aircraft and missiles. Under a 1968 MOU, Belgium, Canada, Denmark, Germany, Greece, Italy, the Netherlands, Norway and the US have participated in this cooperative program. Although the governing MOU predates the Arms Export Control Act, Congress has specifically authorized continued US participation in this successful cooperative program. SeaSparrow production has been completed, and the program is now in the support stage. All US NATO SeaSparrow systems are being upgraded to support the new

Panavia Tornado

The military insignia of the countries which currently fly the Panavia Tornado (*above right, left to right*): the Federal Republic of Germany, Italy, Oman, Saudi Arabia and the United Kingdom.

At right: The Tornado production line in the final assembly hall at Warton Aerodome, Lancashire, UK. A very 'handy' multi-purpose fighter/attack aircraft, the 'swing-wing' Tornado is 54 feet, nine and one-half inches long and has a wingspan of 45 feet, seven inches when fully extended, and 28 feet, 2 inches when fully swept in against the rear wing surfaces.

Above, opposite: A British Tornado, fresh off the assembly line. The Tornado can do Mach 2.2 at altitude, has two Mauser 27mm cannons as standard armament, and in its multi-purpose role, can accept an extremely wide range of 'optional' munitions, including rockets, bombs, electronic warfare devices and extra fuel tanks.

Below, opposite: A brand-new West German Marineflieger (naval air component) Tornado in its preflight prep stage sets on the pavement outside of its hangar at the Luftwaffe Weapon Conversion Unit. Note the Marineflieger insignia just ahead of this plane's forward wing.

RIM-7M missiles. The RIM-7H missile, currently being used by NATO, is not interoperable with the new upgraded system. RIM-7H assets are being maintained in the US to support NATO requirements.

CODEVELOPMENT AND/OR COPRODUCTION BY THE US AIR FORCE WITH ALLIES

Joint Surveillance and Target Attack Radar System (Joint STARS). The US Air Force and Army are developing the Joint Surveillance and Target Attack Radar System (Joint STARS) for multimode surveillance and target attack. Its range and accuracy are tailored for use by both Army and Air Force in attacking stationary or moving targets throughout the enemy first and second echelons.

Similarly, France is developing Orchidee, a heli-borne moving target indicator (MTI) surveillance radar system. The UK is currently evaluating proposals for Castor, an MTI System for Corps use.

NATO is seeking to determine the requirements of other interested nations and to promote interoperability of these national programs. Two NATO Staff Targets (NSTs) have been written for a Standoff Surveillance and Target Acquisition System (SOSTAS) by NATO working groups. One of these NSTs is from an air forces perspective and the other from an army perspective. The next step, which began in January 1986, is to develop NATO Staff Requirements based on the NSTs. In addition, a project group has been established to determine interoperability standards for data exchange between surveillance ground stations operated by various NATO countries.

Joint Tactical Fusion Program (JTFP). The JTFP is developing an automated system that will rapidly receive, correlate, store and disseminate enemy target data from a large number of near-real-time, multidiscipline sensors. This data will be used in the battle execution process by both air and ground commanders and their staffs. The Army uses the All Source Analysis System (ASAS), and the Air Force system is the Enemy Situation Correlation Element (ENSCE); both systems are being developed using lessons learned in the development of the Limited Operational Capability Europe (LOCE) and the Limited Enemy Situation Correlation Element (LENSCE). The JTFP is employing both evolutionary concepts and pre-planned product improvement techniques in the development of the ASAS/ENSCE. The LOCE, which will be replaced by the ASAS/ENSCE, is a candidate system for use in development of the Battlefield Information Collection and Exploitation System (BICES) concept, currently being developed by the NATO Tri-Service Group on Communications and Electronic Equipment.

Airbase Recovery Techniques. The US and Germany signed a Memorandum of Understanding in December 1984 for the evaluation of the German STABO submunition, the US BLU-106B Boosted Kinetic Energy Penetrator (BKEP) submunition, and runway recovery techniques and equipment. BKEP testing was conducted at the German Weapon Test Range, Meppen, Germany, to determine its effectiveness against aircraft shelters. The STABO tests will be conducted in 1986 at Eglin AFB with the munitions being dispensed against a runway target from the MW-1 equipped Tornado aircraft. Subsequently US and German runway clearing and repair equipment and techniques will be demonstrated using the damaged runway. The demonstration under realistic conditions will provide an opportunity to assess the most effective runway clearing/repair procedures for use in Europe.

Aircraft Flight Control Concepts. A Memorandum of Understanding for research into advanced flight control systems was entered into between the USAF and Germany in 1979. Germany is investigating task-oriented-handling qualities of various direct-force-control modes in order to develop a technology data base from which handling qualities criteria can be defined for new control concepts. The US is conducting theoretical and experimental studies to support a continuous effort to revise and update the Military Flying Qualities Specification. Preliminary and final results as well as information on analytical tools developed during the program are being exchanged. This ongoing program will be extended through 1987.

North Warning System. The US and Canada have negotiated a Memorandum of Understanding to provide for the replacement and improvement of the DEW Line System. The existing 31 DEW Line sites will be replaced by 13 minimally-attended radars (AN/FPS-117) and 39 short-range unattended gap-filler radars yet to be developed. The total projected cost for the North Warning System is approximately $1.25 billion, to be shared between the US and Canada on a percentage basis (60/40, respectively).

Low-Cost Powered Dispenser. A Memorandum of Understanding on a collaborative feasibility study for a NATO Low-Cost Powered Dispenser (LOCPOD) with the air forces of Canada, Italy, Spain and the US took effect in October 1985.

LOCPOD fills a NATO military requirement for an off-boresight, short-range, standoff dispenser for attacking fixed targets. Canada is the leader of the LOCPOD Project Group under the NATO Air Force Armaments Group. Two international consortia of companies from each participating country received study contracts in January 1986.

Short-Range Anti-Radiation Missile. The air forces of Belgium, Canada, Germany, Italy, the Netherlands, the UK and the US have signed a Memorandum of Understanding to study the feasibility of a NATO Short-Range Anti-Radiation Missile (SRARM). SRARM is proposed to fill a NATO military requirement for an anti-radiation, self-protection weapon to be employed from the first-line fighter aircraft of the participant nations. The MOU sets the terms and conditions of a multinational collaboration concept exploration of SRARM. Feasibility study contracts were awarded in August 1985 to two consortia made up of industries from each of the participating nations. The studies are scheduled for completion in November 1987.

Variable-Flow-Ducted Rocket Technology. The Governments of France and the United States have agreed to fund and sponsor a program to develop and demonstrate, through test-

Opposite: A fighter pilot inspects the installation of an AIM-9L Sidewinder air-to-air missile on the underwing of his noble steed.

Above: A ground crew services the weapons pylon of their charge. Maintaining NATO's air fleet is a 24-hour-a-day chore.

McDonnell Douglas F-15 Eagle

Above right, left to right: The military insignia for the countries which are currently flying the McDonnell Douglas F-15 Eagle: Israel, Japan, Saudi Arabia and the USA.

At immediate right: A flight of USAFE Eagles of the 32nd Tactical Fighter Squadron based at Soesterberg, Holland flies above the North Sea cloud cover. The Eagle's radar can easily pierce such a barrier, a characteristic which is essential for a fighter operating in the European theater.

The F-15 can do Mach 2.5 at altitude, and its service ceiling is 65,000 feet. Its wingspan is 42 feet 10 inches, and the plane is 63 feet nine inches long. With two Pratt & Whitney F100-PW-100 turbofans cranking out 23,820 pounds of thrust apiece in the F-15A (the F-15C's P&Ws churn out 23,930 apiece), the Eagle is the pride and heart's desire of every eager young fighter jock in the US Air Force—and other air forces as well.

At middle right: Three views of an Eagle. *Above, opposite:* A USAFE F-15 proudly bears its radar-absorbing blue/gray paint job. The F-15 was the first US fighter to receive this color treatment.

Below, opposite: This cutaway view reveals some of the hidden- and not-so-hidden secrets of the F-15 Eagle. *Left to right:* APG-63 combat radar; UHF equipment; avionics bay with automatic direction finding and instrument landing systems; cockpit with Head Up Display; M61 Vulcan cannon with 940 rounds of 20mm ammo; AIM-7 Sparrow AAMs; fuel tanks and fuel lines (in pink); twin Pratt & Whitney turbofans.

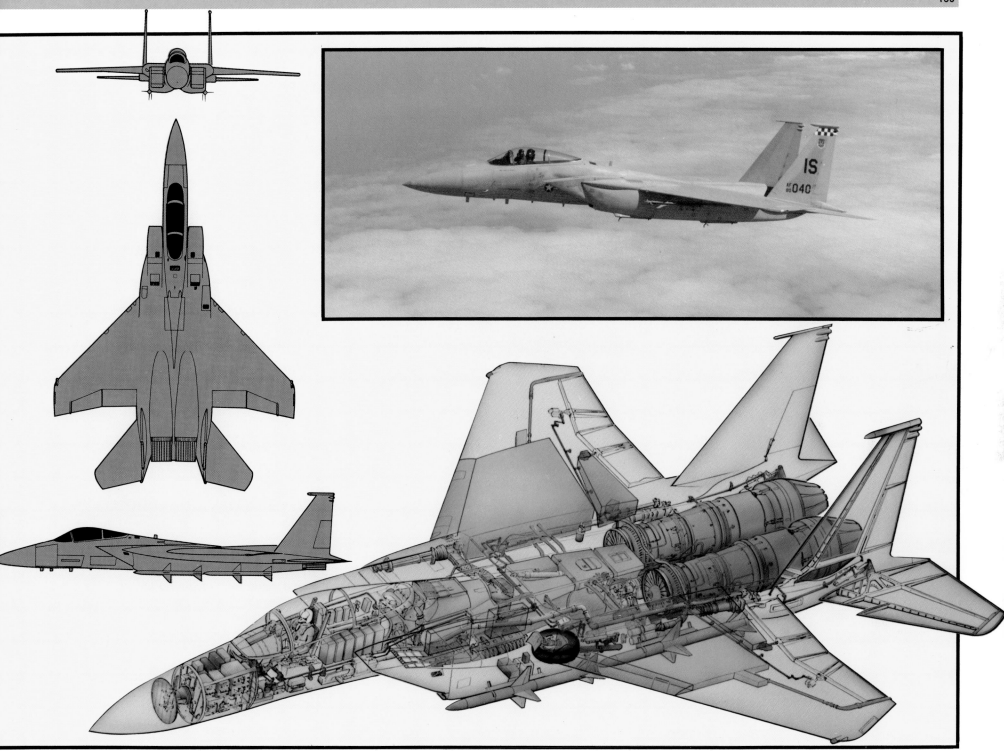

ing, variable-flow-ducted rocket technology. The program, which started in November 1983, entails development of gas generator propellant, development and testing of a ducted rocket insulator, and will culminate in an engine demonstration including booster and ramburner design under specified, simulated flight conditions. The objective of the program is to develop a ducted-rocket concept which is technically superior and less expensive than that which either government might produce alone.

Long-Range Standoff Missile (LRSOM). The NATO Air Force Armaments Group (NAFAG) has approved a NATO Staff Target (NST) for a Long-Range Standoff Missile (LR-SOM). The NST for Long-Range Standoff Missiles identifies a NATO requirement for an air/ground launched, standoff missile for attack of fixed, hardened ground targets, primarily airfields. MOU negotiations by Germany, the UK and the US for feasibility studies of the LRSOM have been completed. The MOU was signed 12 July 1984. Two 15-month study contracts were awarded to two industrial consortia in April 1985.

E-3 Electronic Support Measures (ESM) Cooperative Development. The NATO AEW&C Program Management Agency and appropriate USAF organizations are planning cooperative development actions to integrate a common ESM system into USAF and NATO E-3 aircraft. This project is in an advanced stage, with approvals and US contract award planned for summer 1986. The MOU for this effort includes planning and industrial benefit objectives for production or co-production of the best qualified off-the-shelf ESM system.

COLLECTIVE NATO STANDARDIZATION PROGRAMS

New Secure Voice Technology. The Department of Defense has been working with allied nations to develop a common basis for the next generation of NATO secure voice equipment. The effort has been highly successful, and all potential allied producers have adopted common algorithms and protocols to allow interoperation of their respective designs. The US has accelerated the program by an initiative to loan NATO 360 sets of equipment which are now placed in NATO capitals and military headquarters. These will be replaced by interoperable NATO-procured equipment as it becomes available.

Infrastructure Funded Programs. The primary tasks of the NATO military headquarters are the command and control of the forces provided by the nations, including air defense

forces around the clock and other forces in tension or war, and the preparation in peacetime to execute that task whenever necessary. Acccordingly, there are a number of programs for the support of command and control with communications, data processing, facilities and sensors which simultaneously serve NATO and individual member nations. The number of these projects, which together account for approximately 40 percent of the common-funded Infrastructure budget, is too great to enumerate in this report. Representative examples include the Southern Region Radar Program, a NATO program for improving warning capabilities in the Southern Region which involves collective procurement of eight (plus options) radars for installation in Greece, Italy, Portugal and Turkey. These will furnish information to the host nation as well as the integrated NATO Air Defense System. Another example is the Northern Region Command and Control Information System (CCIS), a NATO program which addresses the needs of Norway, Denmark and several NATO military headquarters in the Northern Region with a single system. A further example in a much larger context, the NATO Integrated Communications System (NICS), represents a continuing effort to provide an Alliance-wide communications system. It is nearing completion of its first stage and will provide a voice and message network that serves all NATO capitals and all NATO military commanders ashore.

In many of these collective programs, the host nation initiates a complementary national program based on the same equipment, thus furthering standardization. Substantial cost-savings accrue through logistics cost reductions for both the Alliance and the host nation.

Above: Checklist in hand, TAC Senior Airman Swasey pauses while preflight checking an F-4 Phantom.

Opposite, left and right: Captain Thomas J Appoloni and TSgt T E Baker, pilot and flight engineer (respectively) prepare to depart for a mission in their MAC UH-1H 'Huey' helicopter.

CHAPTER 8

Allied Contributions to the Common Defense

Secretary of Defense Caspar Weinberger

Adapted from a Report to the United States Congress

Opposite: Frankfurt's Rhein-Main Airport during the air defense presentation for US President Jimmy Carter on 15 July 1978. In wartime, this would be a prime target for the Soviets, and an essential part of joint NATO defense. One plane from the left is the Luftwaffe's Panavia Tornado Prototype 04 with the MW-1 weapon pod. The other aircraft present are (left to right) A USAFE F-111, a USAFE F-15 (one of the famous *Bitburg Eagles*) and a Luftwaffe F-4F.

The commercial side of the airport's business can be seen in the background, with a KLM DC-10 and an Alitalia 747 on the left.

WHAT IS BURDENSHARING?

Our defense arrangements with members of NATO and with Japan rest on formal commitments, freely made by sovereign nations, to contribute by collective efforts to our common security. Alliances, like other agreements, remain healthy so long as they respond to shared national interests. They remain acceptable to members so long as risks and responsibilities are—and are perceived as being—equitably shared. The contributions of partners include both material (quantifiable) factors as well as intangible (eg political) factors, as when governments persevere in policies serving overall security interests in the face of competing domestic and international pressures.

POLITICAL ASPECTS

Any assessment of burdensharing must include an examination of the political environment in which allied governments operate. We continue to share with our allies a common perception of the serious threat that the Soviet Union and its military buildup poses to Alliance security. However, there are understandable differences among the allies as to the most appropriate way to meet the Soviet challenge. These differences arise not only by virtue of history and culture, but also because of geography.

Because their homeland is the potential battlefield, the Europeans' sense of the risks of conflict is more immediate than our own or the Japanese, and the public desire for an easing of

USAF officers in the Air Force Officer Exchange Program are assigned on a reciprocal basis with the air forces of the United Kingdom, France, Spain, Belgium, the Netherlands, Norway, Denmark, Turkey, Jordan and West Germany. A participant in this program is USAF Major Thomas Schmitt (in Luftwaffe orange, *above*—with (l to r) 1st Lt Gerd Becker (his plane's navigator) and Senior Cadet Uwe Dorn-Vogler (his copilot)—in Luftwaffe flight jacket, *far right:* and *at opposite*—with Colonel Dieter Kellein, Commander of the LTG (Luftwaffe Air Transport Wing) 61).

While he is with the Luftwaffe, Major Schmitt is fully considered a Luftwaffe officer especially if Germany were to go to war. His aircraft is a German C-160 Transall (in background *far right* and *opposite*), the Luftwaffe's mainstay tactical transport having a maximum payload capacity of 93 troops, or 81 paratroopers, or 62 stretcher cases.

East-West tensions is more widespread. Families divided by the East-West border have different perceptions and different priorities for East-West rapprochement. And Europe generally tends to attach greater importance to expanding East-West trade.

With these factors in mind, we must regard the leadership that European governments have provided and their successes in support of Alliance defense policies as very real contributions to burdensharing. Differences in perspective that sometimes lead the allies to take independent positions have not marred a record of cooperation that is, on the whole, remarkably good (and surely the envy of any other Alliance system).

An important ongoing success in political burdensharing is the unity and resolve the European allies have shown in staying on course for the deployment of longer-range intermediate-range nuclear forces (LRINF) in the absence of an arms control agreement obviating the need for such deployment. Soviet diplomatic pressures, a massive Soviet effort to influence European public opinion and even openly enunciated threats have not derailed the NATO 'two-track' decision

Above: An RAF Hawk jet trainer/ground attack aircraft flies above the British seacoast, giving us a glimpse of the jet's two AIM-9L Sidewinder close range AAMs, and its 30mm Aden gun's red barrel protruding from its gun pod. The Hawk has been flown since 1979 by the RAF's aerobatic team, the Red Arrows; is currently being used by the RAF as an advanced trainer at RAF Valley; and is active as a weapons trainer/ground attack plane at RAF Brawdy and RAF Chivenor.

Opposite: A Konincklijk Marine (Royal Dutch Navy) P-3 Orion ASW patrol plane hunts for periscopes and radar blips over the North Sea. P-3s have an onboard computer to process and discern the data input from their sophisticated Anti-Submarine Warfare (ASW) sensors—many of which can be seen under this plane's belly as the various interesting bulges, scalloped areas, rods, probe and pylon. P-3s are in service with some nine air forces around the world, including that of the US Navy. Armed with mines and depth bombs (and armable with torpedoes and missiles), the P-3 can spot and, if necessary 'put a few screen doors in,' most any submarine.

of December 1979. The public outcry that greeted the first deliveries at the end of 1983 has only partly subsided, and the political risks faced by the European leaders most directly concerned remains substantial. INF remains a marked demonstration of political courage.

Moreover, with the Soviet occupation of Afghanistan, it is well to recall that our allies took steps to impose political and economic costs on the Soviet Union for its invasion there and that European and Japanese leaders greeted its sixth anniversary with renewed condemnations. Our allies have also taken firm measures in response to Soviet support for repression in Poland. The allies firmly supported the President in his talks with General Secretary Gorbachev.

European assistance in the Middle East (mine clearing the Red Sea and providing peacekeeping forces, for instance) and elsewhere and Japan's increasing economic development assistance, bespeaks an increasing awareness that our defense efforts must be complementary even outside the Atlantic area in order to maximize our common security.

We believe that we will continue to make progress in obtaining important Alliance capability improvements as long as we focus attention on the objective need for such improvements. Achieving US security goals would cost much more if the NATO Alliance and our partnership with Japan were permitted to become weak as a result of divisive arguments over defense burdensharing. Unilateral pronouncements by the United States on the extent to which our allies are or are not sharing the burden are not an effective formula for encouraging improved allied efforts. Our positive leadership has always been, and will remain, a better means to ensure the adequacy of our common defense effort.

Defense analysts do not have a single, universally accepted formula for calculating each country's 'fair share' of the collective defense burden. Any such calculation would have to take account of, and weigh, the many disparate factors that together determine the level of a nation's defense effort. The task is more complicated than simply identifying which factors to count and deciding how each should be weighed relative to the others. While many components of defense effort are measurable, others are much more subjective in nature and do not readily lend themselves to quantification.

The US Effort. Based on the major quantifiable measures examined, the United States appears to be contributing somewhat more than its fair share of the NATO and Japan total. For example, the US defense/GDP (C1) and defense/prosperity

index share ratios are 1.41 and 1.10, respectively. The ratios for active duty manpower/population and active and reserve manpower/population also exceed the 1.0 norm. Of all the indicators considered, only in division equivalents and aircraft do the US ratios drop below 1.0. When taking into account our historical role in NATO and the intangible benefits that accrue to the United States, our allies might argue that we are getting full value for the extra effort we appear to be expending and that our leadership role obligates us to do more than simply achieve our statistically computed fair share.

Allied Efforts. The non-US NATO allies as a group appear to be shouldering roughly their fair share of the NATO and Japan defense burden. For example, the weighted-average ratio of their defense/prosperity index shares is 1.10, while their defense/GDP shares ratio is .79 and all of their remaining ratios exceed 1.0, some by a wide margin.

Important differences emerge, however, when the results for individual countries are compared. Some of the allies appear to be doing more than their statistically computed share. Other NATO nations seem statistically to be doing substantially less than their fair share.

Japan, the only non-NATO country considered in this analysis, ranks last or close to last on most performance measures compared to its ability to contribute—and thus appears to be doing far less than its fair share. Japan recognizes this obligation and has the second highest percentage change in defense spending from 1971–1984. Moreover, Prime Minister Nakasone's Cabinets have authorized defense increases from 1983–1986 at approximately five percent annual real growth over almost all government spending. The US is encouraging the Japanese to increase their contributions to defense even further.

Germany feels that its economic assistance to Berlin and support for the Berlin garrisons, which are not considered 'defense expenditures' under NATO's accounting rules, contribute significantly to the Alliance defense effort in the broadest sense of the word. If included, these expenditures would increase Germany's defense spending total by around 25 percent.

Defense related costs, such as real estate provided for forward-deployed forces and some host nation support expenditures, also are not counted as defense spending under the NATO definition. The current market value of the real estate made available to allied forces stationed in Germany, for example, has been estimated at around $16 billion.

Similar to USAFE, the US Air Force Pacific Air Forces (PACAF) is an important contributor to the allied interlocking defense chain in the Pacific arena. *Above:* Two PACAF pilots inform ground crew chief Sergeant Judy K Busselman of a malfunction in their F-4E Phantom—a popular plane for PACAF.

Opposite: USAF F-15A Eagle aircraft are refueled—at Chitose AB, Japan—during Exercise Cope North 84-1. F-15J Eagles, from the Japanese Air Self Defense Force, are parked in the background. Specifically, the planes in this photo are (left to right): JASDF F-4, US Air Force (PACAF) F-15A, JASDF F-15J, JASDF F-15J, JASDF F-104, JASDF F-15J, US Air Force (PACAF) F-15A, US Air Force (PACAF) F-15A. Japan, a non-NATO contributor to the allied international defense effort, contributes something on the order of 4.1 percent of the combined NATO/non-NATO allied military airpower.

Some European nations, especially Germany, incur additional expenses by hardening or building redundancy into civil projects with potential military applications. Examples include roads, pipelines and civilian communication systems. Many of these expenditures cannot be reported under NATO's defense accounting criteria.

The value of civilian assets (e g , trucks) that are designed for military use in time of war likewise cannot be counted as defense expenditures. Yet these assets contribute directly to NATO's and Japan's military capabilities and reduce the amount these nations and the United States might otherwise have to spend on defense. This is particularly the case for Germany, which has undertaken a significant program to register civilian assets that would be used by the Bundeswehr and allied forces in wartime.

It is important to emphasize that there are not single, comprehensive output indicators that fully reflect all of the factors that constitute military capability. The material presented here is intended to provide a thumbnail sketch of each country's force contributions by highlighting a few key static indicators that are widely accepted within the defense analysis community. The data used for these displays are based largely on US estimates and incorporate country responses to the NATO Defense Planning Questionnaire for those nations that participate in NATO's coordinated defense planning process.

The ADE is a relative measure of effectiveness of ground forces based on quantity and quality of major weapons. This measure is an improvement over simple accounts of combat units and weapons; however, it does not take into account such factors as ammunition availability, logistical support, training, communications and morale. At the present time there is no single indicator that incorporates these additional factors.

The non-US nations combined account for 59 percent of the ADEs of the NATO members and Japan while the United States supplies the remaining. The allied contribution drops to 55 percent if Japan is excluded.

Tonnage is a static measure of aggregate fleet size. For most purposes, it provides a more meaningful basis for comparison than do simple tallies of ships. The use of tonnage alone does not, however, provide any indication of the numbers of weapons aboard ships or of the weapons' effectiveness or reliability. Nor does the measure take account of the less tangible ingredients of combat effectiveness, such as personnel training and morale. Consequently, tonnage data should be considered as giving an indication of naval potential.

The proportion of fighter/interceptor, attack, bomber and tactical reconnaissance aircraft in the NATO and Japanese inventories of major powers are: United States, 43 percent; France, 9.3 percent; United Kingdom, 9.2 percent; Federal Republic of Germany, 8.7 percent; Italy, 5.9 percent; Turkey, 4.4 percent and Japan, 4.1 percent. Trainer aircraft considered to be combat capable are included in the equipment counts; electronic warfare aircraft are not.

Although no single non-US nation accounts for more than 10 percent of the NATO and Japan total, the combined holdings of these countries represent 59 percent of the total. Excluding Japan, the non-US NATO share drops slightly, to 55 percent.

With 43 percent of its inventory consisting of new-generation aircraft and the remaining 57 percent comprising current-generation equipment, the US Air Force is further along in its aircraft modernization program than are the air forces of the other NATO members. For those countries, new-generation aircraft constitute 20 percent of their combined air-

Opposite, left to right: An RAF Hercules and a Luftwaffe C-160 Transall wait on the ramp as a US Air Force C-130 Hercules taxis into the parking area at RAF Wildenrath, West Germany, during Reforger 84. Though having approximately the same length and width dimensions, the Hercules is the heavier lifter—by approximately 33,602 pounds of maximum payload capability.

Above: Looking terribly like Don Rickles (but no doubt much more polite), a German officer salutes multinational dignitaries as they disembark a German barge which was used to view the Rhine River crossing operation conducted by joint British and German forces during the Reforger 84 NATO war games' Autumn Forge phase.

Opposite: Medical airlift during the Reforger 86 international military maneuvers: Captain McGuire, NATO medical crew director (left); Captain Daniels (middle), flight nurse; and LTC Doench, doctor, discuss procedures to be used for the evacuation of wounded personnel by means of the German C-160 Transall medium transport plane.

Above: A photoportrait of LTC/Doctor Doench, a doctor with the German Air Support Command in Muenster, Federal Republic of Germany.

Above, left: Reforger 84 saw another answer to the Medevac question—A1C Gregory B West (left) and SSgt G M Reed (middle) provide medical attention to an injured airman at a simulated crash scene. In this exercise, the wounded would be medivated to the nearest medical facility via the Luftwaffe UH-1D helicopter in the background.

The ubiquitous UH-1 was named Iroquois, but is known universally as 'Huey' because of the acronym formed by its designation. In service with armies and air forces throughout the world, the Huey originated with Bell Helicopter in the United States and was later produced in Germany by Dornier.

craft holdings, whereas current-generation models account for 67 percent and older planes for the remaining 13 percent. That picture, too, will change over the coming years, as the major modernization programs now underway within most of the allied air forces near completion. As a result, by the late 1980s, new-generation aircraft will constitute a sizable share of the allied inventory with few older-model planes remaining except in the southern flank countries.

In the NATO civil planning process (which includes integral participation by US officers charged with the implementation of carefully orchestrated inter-agency guidance derived from the Departments of State, Defense, Commerce, Transportation, Energy and Agriculture, as well as the National Communications System and the Federal Emergency Management Agency), NATO civil planners are looking beyond the finite requirements of the Rapid Reinforcement Plan (RRP) to questions of supply, resupply and sustainability. Planners are making a concerted effort to examine total civil and military requirements in order to ensure that all facets of civil emergency planning are satisfactorily accomplished.

These include (1) maintenance of the machinery of government and its capability to deal with a crisis and assurance of its continued functioning in wartime, (2) support and protection of the civil populations and (3) civil support to the members of the Alliance and to the military by means of mobilization and use of allied civil resources and infrastructure. This broader look at civil requirements, as well as at purely military requirements, is essential in helping to underpin the political will of the Alliance and to prevent any distraction from mobilization in a crisis by 'butter versus guns' arguments.

Specifically under the CDI program, and using the existing organizational structure of NATO, the civil emergency planners have undertaken the following:

Continued efforts to obtain the commitment of civilian passenger aircraft to further support the reinforcement of the European community.

Continued efforts to obtain the commitment of long-range cargo-capable civil aircraft of member nations and investigation of methods to optimize the use of combination passenger/cargo aircraft.

Efforts to revise restrictive safety criteria that would allow highly capable new twin-engine civil aircraft (Boeing 767, Airbus A-300 and Airbus A-310) to be used for Alliance airlift.

Examination of the possible use of civil short takeoff and landing (STOL) aircraft and civil helicopters in support of the needs of members of the Alliance and military operations.

The development of coordinated civil plans for air movements in support of the military and to meet the needs of Alliance members' civil aviation services in crisis and war.

Completion of allied arrangements for reception and onward movement of ammunition, including plans to modify or waive national legislation regarding treatment of hazardous material.

Assessment of total (civil and military) fuel, oil and lubricant demand in crisis and war, determination of shortfalls and development of inland transportation plans including the use of civilian facilities and equipment.

NATO member nations depend upon the availability of civilian transport aircraft that can be used for military airlift— thereby increasing military capabilities without increasing expenditures, and providing a very useful emergency back-up force.

Such civilian aircraft as the Boeing 747-200F heavy-lift freighter *shown opposite and above* (which is capable of carrying a 250,000-pound cargo for more than 3000 miles), would come in mighty handy. . . . in the event of war. Similar transports flying for Cargolux, in Luxembourg, fly the heaviest cargo loads of any aircraft in the world, regularly carrying cargo loads approaching 900,000 pounds.

WARTIME HOST NATION SUPPORT

The structure and content of WHNS arrangements vary widely from country to country. Nevertheless, some generic types of arrangements exist with numerous allies.

The Collocated Operating Bases (COB) program was developed in the early 1970s as a follow-on project for support of US reinforcing air squadrons. The program continues to offer substantial savings to the US. Over 70 bases in Europe have been identified to support USAF US-based reinforcements in addition to the existing 22 main operating bases (MOBs) and six standby dispersal bases (SDBs).

Similar arrangements also exist for wartime operations of US naval aviation, including Marine aircraft groups (MAGs) and maritime patrol aircraft (MPA) squadrons. COBs and similar bases require considerable US and host nation planning and investment in peacetime. Since COBs are normally active peacetime bases of the host nation's air force, the host nation would provide virtually all the necessary infrastructure, base operating support and airfield services. Construction of additional facilities needed to support US squadrons (e g aircraft shelters, runway repair material, additional quarters) is funded through the NATO common infrastructure program, by the host nation, or jointly by the host nation and the US.

Several WHNS agreements call for host nations to provide organized military and civilian units to provide combat service support to US forces. An example is the German WHNS agreement which calls for some 93,000 military reservists in 173 units to perform wartime logistics functions for US forces. These include transportation, casualty evacuation and NBC defense battalions; security and maintenance and service companies; airfield damage repair platoons; medical squadrons and escort batteries. These reserve units also have their own command and control structure. The US and Germany are sharing the costs of equipping these units and providing the necessary infrastructure for them. In addition, Germany has agreed to provide a substantial number of civilian personnel for other support tasks.

CHAPTER 9
The Scenario:
Day One
by Bill Yenne

Opposite: **The Soviet routes of attack on the first day of World War III (clockwise from upper left) might include air attacks on Iceland, Norway and the UK; heavy armor thrust into Central Europe via West Germany; air attacks on Southern Europe from Warsaw Pact countries and from bases in Libya; air and armor attack on Turkey with heavy armor pincer on Istanbul; armor attack on Iran and on Pakistan from bases in Afghanistan.**

ATTACK

If World War III is fought with conventional weapons it will have to start on the Central Front somewhere between Lubeck and the Austrian frontier. The Warsaw Pact will have to address the Central Front in any scenario because western Europe is the prize and the Federal Republic of Germany is the gateway to that prize.

In his 1978 bestseller, *The Third World War,* Sir John Hackett predicted that the war would start in August 1985 on the Central Front. He was wrong about the year, but that was probably the only thing about his premise that will prove incorrect. Soviet forces will probably attack in the summer because of the weather, although as the all-weather capability of their air forces improves a winter attack can't be ruled out. The massed armor that the Soviets possess can move almost as easily in snow as on bare ground, but in springtime flooded marsh and swampland might present a problem. Europe is al-

most always partly cloudy, but winter is almost always *mostly* cloudy, so a summer scenario seems the most likely.

The attack will come on a broad front in the wee hours of a summer morning. The backbone of the Soviet blitzkreig, like the Nazi blitzkreigs of 1939-40, will be tanks. In this case *tens of thousands* of tanks! They will pour into West Germany from the German Democratic Republic and possibly from Czechoslovakia, and their immediate objective will be to reach and hold a line roughly 80 miles from the present borders within eight hours. The Warsaw Pact forces will include mostly Soviet troops, but other nationalities will be accorded at least token representation.

The tanks and armored personnel carriers will be supported by tactical airpower and large numbers of helicopter gunships such as the new Kamov Hokum, or the old standby Mil Mi-24 Hind and Mi-28 Havoc. The Warsaw Pact air forces will fly immediate, deep interdiction strikes against *every* USAFE, Luftwaffe and other NATO air base in West Germany and the

Netherlands. The attacks will be timed to coincide with the massed ground attack and will be designed to destroy the bulk of NATO's airpower in the war's first minutes and to render the air bases unusable for reinforcements that might be sent in from the United States or the UK. Whether these strikes are successful will depend on the state of NATO's early warning and anti-aircraft capability. There will be less than 15 minutes warning, so false moves could prove deadly for NATO airpower.

Other Warsaw Pact air strikes will be flown against NATO ground troop concentrations, but strikes on nonmilitary targets will be limited to those which would not be useful to an occupation force.

The first day's overall objective on the Central Front will be to destroy as much NATO airpower as possible and to put War-saw Pact ground forces within sight of Frankfurt and Hamburg.

On the Northern Front, the situation will be much more fluid and dependent upon airborne forces rather than armor. Soviet tanks simply couldn't penetrate more than a tiny part of Norway overland. A seaborne invasion would be much too slow, so the Russians will use airborne forces against Norway and Denmark, as the Germans did in 1940.

While ground troops *will* take that small slice of northern Norway that is immediately available, airborne and helicopter-borne troops will depart Murmansk, round the Nordkapp, and land at all of Norway's northern ports from Hammerfest to Trondheim. Supported by tactical airpower and perhaps by heavy bomber attacks as well, these landings will be aimed at capturing these ports, as well as preventing their use for counterattacks against Murmansk.

Opposite: **Here they come! A field full of Soviet T-72 tanks and infantry comple-ment crush German soil underfoot.**

Above middle left: **An A-10 tank buster will find a 'target rich' environment, while American M-1 tanks (above), with their huge, barn door-sized armor plates would have their work cut out for them.**

Right: The column of enemy tanks was still several miles away when the attacking aircraft began its firing run. Its Forward Looking Infrared (FLIR) was already tracking their heat signatures. Less than three seconds later, with the aircraft still safely out of range the missiles slammed into their targets with uncanny accuracy.

One of the most awesomely effective weapons ever developed for Close Air Support/Battlefield Air Interdiction, the Hypervelocity Missile (HVM) weapon system was designed to deliver a maximum firepower at a cost far below anything in the current inventory. A product of the Missiles Division of LTV Missiles and Electronics Group, HVM is a masterpiece of simplicity and ingenuity. It carries no warhead, relying instead on its blistering 5000-foot-per-second speed to blast a penetrator rod through heavy multi-plate armor, even at highly oblique angles at extreme range.

Its guidance system is a simple CO_2 laser, mounted on the aircraft. With only an aft-looking receiver on the missile, the amount of expensive 'throwaway' hardware is held to an absolute minimum. And because HVM is a 'wooden round' with no warhead, storage and handling are simpler, safer and cheaper.

Opposite: US Air Force Tactical Command F-15s based in Iceland would lift off to face the oncoming air attack onslaught. *Overleaf:* Soviet Bear bombers regularly stray into NATO airspace near Iceland in peacetime, no doubt in preparation for wartime 'straying'—for purposes of destroying Allied shipping, reinforcing Cuba, decoying NATO air defense, etcetera. The F-15s would not be nearly so friendly then.

Air attacks from Murmansk will be made against ports south of Trondheim, such as Bergen and possibly Oslo, but airborne invasions will probably not be attempted until the ports and air bases north of Trondheim are securely under Soviet control.

The main Soviet air attacks against Denmark and southern Norway will probably be made from Poland and East Germany, and the decision to attempt an airborne attack on a target such as Copenhagen will probably await the outcome of the first 12 hours of activity on the Central Front.

Any attacks made against Norway will also probably judiciously avoid violation of Swedish air space. Sweden, like Finland, is neutral and has no obligation to fight alongside NATO, but it would fight ferociously if its neutrality were to be violated. Sweden has a very well trained and well equipped air force which could not be overcome without cost. Engaging it would certainly delay a Warsaw Pact offensive on the Northern Front, so it will be avoided if at all possible.

Beyond Norway on the Northern Front are the icy waters of the Norwegian Sea and what NATO planners call the Greenland-Iceland-United Kingdom (GIUK) Gap. Into this gap will go the Soviet Bears and Backfire bombers which have been plying this air space for years enroute to Cuba and in anticipation of the eventual war. These long range bomber and reconnaissance patrols through the GIUK Gap would, in wartime, play serious havoc with NATO shipping on the North Atlantic. US Air Force Tactical Air Command fighters based at Keflavik airport near Reykjavik, Iceland and RAF Tornado ADVs based in the UK could in turn play serious havoc with the Bears and Backfires, so it's not unlikely that Soviet plans

Above: A Panavia Tornado Air Defense Variant (ADV) interceptor, furious as the wind itself, could make the crew of a Soviet bomber sorry that they ever sought to mess with this twister's home turf, Great Britain.

Opposite: Two Tornado strike fighters from RAF Honington blast toward hypothetical Soviet armor in Norway, as at exactly that moment, their base may be turned into a mass of rubble and craters by Backfire bombers.

will call for an attack on Iceland. Destroying Keflavik would remove a serious problem, but an airborne attack to *seize* Keflavik would provide an extremely valuable base. Such an attack would be costly because Iceland is four times as far from Murmansk than from the UK. If, however, it were to be attacked from newly-won bases in Norway, the task would be easier.

After Germany, the most important targets for Warsaw Pact airpower will be in the UK. These will also be very heavily defended and the Soviets will undoubtedly think long and hard about whether to launch a second Battle of Britain. Because of the potential use of the UK to base long range strategic bombers such as B-52s and B-1s as well as FB-111s, the Soviet air planners may have no choice but to attack UK air bases. Had the Germans conducted such attacks properly, the *second* world war might have evolved differently.

A second choice that Soviet air planners will confront if they decide to attack the UK will be whether to go in from Poland across Denmark and the North Sea or whether to brave a much greater distance but less opposition and come in from Murmansk in the north.

On the Southern Front, air attacks against northern Italy are probable, but would involve the Soviet attackers having to violate Austrian and/or Yugoslav air space. Whether they chance such a move depends on the political situation and whether Austrians and Yugoslavs acquiesce to or militarily oppose such a move.

Attacks against Greece or Turkey are possible and Istanbul's precious waterways have long been coveted by the Russians. Istanbul would be virtually indefensible against a determined Soviet pincer that involved a land invasion from Bulgaria coupled with an amphibious landing from the Black Sea.

Above: **A soot-blackened and hastily camouflaged USAFE guard listens for the scream of an Eagle—or the whacking echo of Soviet attack helicopters from his defensive position near the perimeter of Bitburg AFB.**

Opposite: **McDonnell Douglas C-17s deploy equipment via the Low Altitude Parachute Extraction System (LAPES), somewhere in the parched dryness of the Middle East. Now under development, the C-17 will enter squadron service with MAC in the early 1990s.**

Overleaf: **The US Marines—an important part of any action in the Middle East because of their fast deployment capability—would counterattack against the Soviet drive across Iran toward the Persian Gulf. For once, the Ayatollas manage a kind word for the 'infidels.'**

In the central Mediterranean, the Libyan bases at Tripoli and Bengazi are de facto Soviet bases today, and in wartime they'll provide a key staging area for attacks on Italy and Spain and other targets on NATO's southern flank. The Libyan bases would, however, be the most vulnerable in the Soviet arsenal.

The Soviets may or may not decide on simultaneous moves in the Middle East, such as an attack on Pakistan from Afghanistan or a move to seize the Persian Gulf oil fields. In all probability, these attacks would come later in the conflict after the situation in Europe—particularly on the Central Front—had developed a somewhat predictable momentum. If attacked on all three European fronts, NATO would have little ability to divert forces to face a Soviet Middle East attack. Thus, an invasion of this region could be undertaken almost at leisure.

In summary, the Soviet attack will come on all three European fronts simultaneously because of Soviet numerical superiority in manpower and weapons. To attack on only one front would allow the NATO defenders to concentrate their forces. The main thrust will, of course, come on the Central Front.

Above: A British counterattack on European soil: An RAF Harrier empties its Matra 155 rocket pods.

Opposite: The attack/counterattack scheme for the European theatre—those tangled lines of attack represent many casualties, accidents, minor triumphs and outright victories—one could call them 'lines of fatigue.'

COUNTERATTACK

NATO forces are committed to defense and could not be deployed until a Warsaw Pact attack, so for NATO air crews it is a question of how fast can one be in the air and what will be left of the base when one is lucky enough to return.

NATO interceptors—USAFE F-15s and Luftwaffe Tornados, for instance—will go to work immediately trying to shoot down Warsaw Pact fighter bombers and bombers. The story will be the same from the GIUK Gap, where the F-15s will be TAC and the Tornados RAF, to the Mediterranean, where the defenders will be Italian Tornados, Spanish F-18s and American F-14 Tomcats from US Navy carriers.

On the Central Front there will be so many aircraft flying and fighting at incredible speeds that collisions and accidental shootdowns will be inevitable. It will be a veritable hornet's nest in which the attrition rate will be nothing short of horrible.

Closer to the ground, attack aircraft such as RAF Harriers, Luftwaffe Alpha Jets and USAFE A-10 Warthogs will go to work on the invading tanks. It will be, as military planners say, a *'target rich'* environment: there will be so many tanks that a Warthog could hit one with *every* shell from its formidable 30mm cannon and not hit them all. The attack aircraft will share the lower airspace with attack helicopters such as the US Army's AH-64 Apache, which will also be attacking Warsaw Pact ground forces fast and feverishly.

Above and behind it all, US Air Force and NATO E-3 Sentry AWACS aircraft will monitor the complex and fast-moving air situation, directing attack aircraft to targets and interceptors to intruding airplanes. Because the AWACS aircraft will be prime targets, NATO fighter aircraft will have to be diverted to protect them.

Like the AWACS, which will set up 'stations' high over Belgium and the North Sea, aerial refueling tankers will have to

establish refueling tracks wherein NATO combat aircraft can refuel without returning to base—a base which is very likely to be under attack.

Air superiority over the battlefield and destruction of enemy ground forces will be the first mission of NATO airpower. Next comes the question of counterattack. NATO in peacetime is very nervous about planning attacks on Warsaw Pact supply lines and air bases near the front in East Germany, Czechoslovakia, Poland and Hungary. It will, however, be a military ne-

Left: Survivors of a deadly day, these Bitburg Eagle drivers would be very weary. They figure themselves to be the best fighter pilots in the whole world; in World War III, they would have to be.

Above: US Air Force Tactical Air Command Eagles tote a load of grief for attacking forces—and this pilot is every bit as intent on the invaders as his masked face looks.

cessity to hit hard and fast against such targets, in East Germany at the very least. To allow Warsaw Pact forces to destroy NATO airfields in West Germany while avoiding a similar attack on East Germany would be to invite disaster. When these attacks come, they will be flown by F-16s and Tornados based in Germany, as well as by USAFE F-111s and SAC FB-111s based in the UK.

On the Northern Front, Danish and Norwegian F-16s will be the first line of defense against Soviet warplanes and the Soviet transports that would carry airborne troops. How this defensive operation is handled would write the script for the next step. If the Soviets successfully seize Norwegian air bases, then NATO airpower would have to drop back and vigorously attack those bases with the hope of recapturing them as

Above and opposite: The Luftwaffe's Tornadoes may cross the Elbe and penetrate as far as the Bug to carry the war to the Warsaw Pact.

Below: F-4 Phantoms under a blanket of snow. The one in the foreground is in the conventional camouflage scheme that dates back to the Vietnam War. The one in the background is in the extremely rare mint green scheme.

It is Wisconsin, but it could be the fens of Poland or Norway. The deep interdiction 'Strike Eagle' (*above*) entered service in 1987 under the designation F-15E. Its job: intensive discouragement of hostile troops before they find the road to your door.

Opposite: The US Army uses the Bell AH-1S Huey modernized Cobra attack helicopter and its eight TOW missiles, 2.75-inch rockets and 20mm cannon to 'mop up' after the very potent AH-64 Apache attack helicopter—the Huey's 'mop' is much smaller than that of AH-64.

soon as possible. If they are successfully defended, NATO planners could begin planning for a possible air attack to neutralize Murmansk.

In Iceland, NATO will be defending against bombers that have flown longer distances and which will be easier to detect, but the situation could by no means be taken for granted. By sending Murmansk-based Backfires and Bears to attack Iceland and Scotland, the Soviets would tie down a large number of NATO interceptors.

On the Southern Front, NATO forces will face the same dilemma about violating Austrian and Yugoslav air space that the Warsaw Pact air forces do. The question will have a political answer.

Above: A German officer directs the un-loading of British equipment from a barge. Small, hard to hit and relatively speedy land vehicles such as these 'jeeps' are a transportation premium in an environment of heavy equipment casualties.

Right: Medevac Transall airlifters bath-ed in light the color of a contusion are hurriedly loaded with casualties.

Opposite: The MAC airlift breaks through, even amid the virtual blizzard of tactical projectiles and combat planes that thicken the Northern European skies this day. The question is—are these C-17s and their armored units led by M-1 tanks too late to recapture this hypothet-ical terrain which might be Norway?

Above: This Luftwaffe Tornado is going ship hunting with its Kormoran anti-ship missiles, next-to-fuselage AIM Sidewinders and pylon-mounted electronic reconnaissance pods.

Opposite: Two defenders from the USAFE 50th Security Police Squadron consult with a West German forester upon the probable best place to lay an ambush that in wartime would be set to snare Soviet ground troops.

Defense of Istanbul will be like that of West Germany on a smaller geographical scale and will probably involve NATO's airlift force if a concerted effort is made to launch a ground counterattack.

The Soviet/Libyan bases at Tripoli and Bengazi will almost certainly come under NATO counter air attack immediately. An airborne assault to capture and hold these bases would go a long way toward NATO's being able to achieve air superiority over the Mediterranean early in a conflict.

In the background of all these activities rests the question of whether to attack targets *within the Soviet Union itself.* Certainly there will be important air bases and staging areas, from Riga to Kaliningrad to Minsk, that would be logical targets, as would Murmansk. However, the United States is bound to weigh the probability that the use of its aircraft in such attacks would invite attacks on *its* territory, such as in Alaska, or even against Seattle or Portland. The territory of the UK may or may not be attacked at the outset, but the Soviets will no doubt claim some 'provocation' before they strike *London.*

West Germany will be consumed as a battlefield by this time, so the question of inviting a reprisal is moot. The Luftwaffe's Tornados *could* reach the Soviet Union. The problem arises, however, that in 1941, the Luftwaffe spearheaded a nearly successful invasion of Soviet territory that was *not* militarily provoked. Politically, an attack too deep in the Soviet Union by the Luftwaffe could invite a tactical nuclear war.

At top: Not to be ruled out of any World War III scenario is the US Navy's own 'top gun,' the F-14 Tomcat, a Mach 2.34 fighter armed with much optional kill hardware, including the deadly AIM-54 Phoenix missile, which can make a 'barn door' out of anything that flies.

Above: A 'Wolfpack' crewman from squadron VF-1 hustles by one of the F-14 Tomcats aboard the USS Enterprise during a PACAN alert. After their performance in World War II, carriers became the most important ships in the entire US Fleet, and have been handling heavy peacekeeping and surveillance chores in the Atlantic and the Mediterranean for some time. The US Navy generally keeps two or three carriers attached to its Sixth Fleet in the troubled Mediterranean. Of course, the carriers themselves would be targets, but precisely because carrier-based fighters and fighter-bombers such as F-14s (*right*) and F/A-18 Hornets would bring crushing firepower to bear on hostile forces along NATO's southern front.

CHAPTER 10
The Scenario: Day Two
by Bill Yenne

Well-camouflaged Warsaw Pact troops (*right*) negotiate barbed wire obstacles on an airstrip perimeter, while one of their comrades gives covering fire with his AK-47.

Opposite: **Given their overwhelming numerical superiority, Soviet and Warsaw Pact ground forces have the potential to invade and occupy large slices of territory over a broad front in the first days of a potential conflict. This in turn would force NATO airpower to divert its attention to these areas, and away from the defense of targets on the northern front where physical threat of invasion is less likely. With said air defenses thus thinned, Soviet airpower could attack NATO air and sea supply lanes.**

ATTACK

By the sheer weight of numerical superiority, the Soviet Union stands a *chance* of being able to develop enough momentum in its thrust to overwhelm most of West Germany, the Netherlands and Denmark within a day or two. Munich and Hamburg may be encircled rather than invaded, and Amsterdam may well be bypassed in favor of continuing the momentum of the drive across Belgium into France. The battle plan then would then probably parallel that used by Germany in 1914-18 and again in 1940.

By this stage, air raids against Britain will be common, and the channel ports will be particularly hard hit. France will not enter the war immediately, but will probably find so much of it spilling over into its territory, that it will have to join.

On the Northern Front airborne assaults will have been made against Norway and will perhaps have been attempted

Above: Casualties are offloaded from Luftwaffe C-160s and ferried to already full hospitals aboard US Army litter buses.

Effective and versatile in the Vietnam War, the SLUF (Short Little Ugly Fellow), aka the A-7 Corsair II, is extremely dependable. *Opposite:* In this view, an updated A-7 'Strikefighter' with all-weather strike capability carries its load to an unsuspecting enemy under unfriendly skies.

against the Faeroe and Shetland Islands, as well as against the UK itself.

Having secured some or all of the intended airborne targets, Soviet forces will either find themselves digging in against a fierce counterattack or else isolated and awaiting reinforcement. The primary question will be whether these outposts will be harbingers of bigger Soviet forces arriving on the scene or whether they are expendable diversions.

On the Southern Front, NATO forces will be in a stronger position, except in Turkey. The Libyan bases will be lost and will become key NATO airlift points for troops and supplies moving into Turkey and the Middle East. This, combined with American carrier battle groups, will give NATO the upper edge on air superiority. Soviet airpower based in Bulgaria and Turkey will no doubt make a high priority of sinking American carriers, while NATO airpower will attack Soviet shipping on the Black Sea in an attempt to close off the waterways around Istanbul, if the Soviets succeed in capturing the city.

Above: The RAF Nimrod AWACS aircraft, controversial during its development because of cost overrruns, will ultimately be replaced in RAF service by the Boeing E-3 Sentry AWACS.

A US Army AH-64 primary attack helicopter (*above*) dives to assault an armored column with its tank-scalping 30mm chain gun and 2.75-inch rockets. The Apache is NATO's only all-weather, day or night, adverse conditions attack helicopter.

Above right: These C-130s and C-160s would represent a union of the US/German resupply forces as the NATO powers prepared to mount a savage counteroffensive.

Below right: A 14th TAC Fighter Squadron 1st Lieutenant prepares, like other members of his squadron, to go on a MiG hunt in his F-16. In World War III this hunt might break NATO convention if the MiGs were found within Soviet borders.

Opposite: In our hypothetical scenario, counteroffensive would strike deep and wide. Not only Warsaw Pact countries, but the Soviet Bear itself might bleed, as Russia would risk the loss of its hypocritical 'hands-off' privilege. Such attacks, however, might invite an escalation of the conflict as the Soviets considered a nuclear response to the counterattack.

COUNTERATTACK

Faced with the loss of territory on the Central and Northern Fronts as well as airborne landings throughout Europe, NATO will have a steep climb. Losses will have been high on land and sea, as well as in the air. These will be losses that NATO can ill afford because of its numerical inferiority in most categories of manpower and weaponry.

It may well be that a Warsaw Pact blitzkreig would be so costly that NATO would be unable to fight back after several days of losses. On the other hand, losses may be minimized through a combination of superior weapons and training. Their supply lines cut, the Warsaw Pact's Central Front juggernaut may run out of steam and be cut up and destroyed. NATO airborne troops might recapture lost territory in Norway and Germany and may launch counterthrusts across the former Iron Curtain.

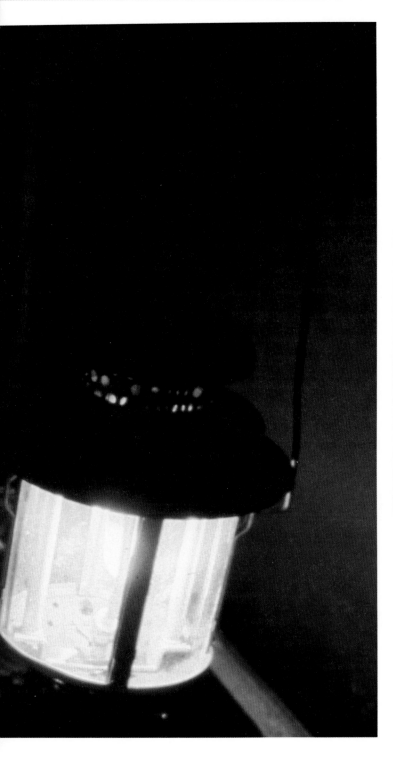

SUMMARY

This two day scenario is pure fiction and supposes the probable course of the opening salvos of World War III *if it remains conventional.* What these pages *do* illustrate is the reason NATO exists and the types of battlefield considerations that NATO's military planners must think about when they select weaponry and outline possible tactics.

The bottom line is that, in order to prevent this scenario, NATO must develop and maintain the type of forces necessary to act it out should the other side decide to take a chance on initiating it.

Above: A ground crew member prepares a very hard used attack/reconnaissance aircraft for yet another mission, as the sun rises ominously in the east.

A Security Police Squadron radio man (*opposite*) hears the news from the front—his unit will be getting a heavy workout if the Reds get restless.

These pages: A camouflage gray RAF air defense Tornado seeks bogeys in an increasingly clear sky. A Soviet Bear may soon be getting its nose swatted—and almost taken off! What will the Warsaw Pact come up with next?

INDEX

GLOSSARY OF ACRONYMS

AAFCE: Allied Air Forces Central Europe
AAM: Air-to-Air Missile
AB: Air Base
ABM: Anti-Ballistic Missile
ACCHAN: Allied Command Channel
ACCS: NATO Air Command and Control System
ACE: Allied Command Europe
ACLANT: Allied Command Atlantic
ADV: Air Defense Variant (Tornado)
AEW: Airborne Early Warning
AEW&C: Airborne Early Warning & Control
AFB: Air Force Base
AFCENT: Allied Forces Central Europe
AFNORTH: Allied Forces Northern Europe
AFSOUTH: Allied Forces Southern Europe
AGM: Air-to-Ground Missile
AIM: Air Intercept Missile
AIRSOUTH: Allied Air Forces Southern Europe
ALCM: Air Launched Cruise Missile
AMRAAM: Advanced Medium Range Air-to-Air Missile
AS: Air Station (smaller version of AB or AFB)
ASRAAM: Advanced Short Range Air-to-Air Missile
AWACS: Airborne Warning and Control Systems
CALIF: Civil Airlift Task Force
CCIS: Northern Region Command and Control Information System
CENTAG: Central Army Group
CINCHAN: Allied Commander in Chief, Channel
COB: Collacated Operating Bases
COMAIRSOUTH: Commander Air South
DEW: Distant Early Warning (northern radar system)
ECM: Electronic Counter Measures
EFA: European Fighter Aircraft

EPG: Independent European Program Group
FIVEATAF: Allied Tactical Air Force, Fifth
FOURATAF: Allied Tactical Air Force, Fourth
GIUK: Greenland-Iceland-United Kingdom gap
GLCM: Ground Launced Cruise Missile
GPS: NAVSTAR Global Positioning System
HAVE QUICK: A US-developed anti-jam voice communication system
HAVE QUICK II: An improved version of HAVE QUICK
HVM: Hypervelocity Missile System (LTV)

IDS: Interdictor Strike (Tornado)
INF: Intermediate-range Nuclear Force aircraft
JASDF: Japanese Air Self-Defense Force
Joint STARS: Joint Surveillance and Target Attack Radar System
JTFP: Joint Tactical Fusion Program
JTIDS: Joint Tactical Information Distribution System
LANDSOUTH: Allied Land Forces Southern Europe
LANDSOUTHEAST: Allied Land Forces southeastern Europe
LRINF: Longer-Range INF
LRSM: Long-Range Standoff Missile

TACTICAL COMBAT AIRCRAFT (Including Spain)

	1984	
	% of NATO & Japan Total	*Rank*
Belgium	2.51%	9
Canada	2.39%	10
Denmark	1.38%	14
France	9.29%	2
Germany	8.73%	4
Greece	4.01%	8
Italy	5.86%	5
Luxembourg	0.00%	16
Netherlands	2.29%	11
Norway	1.47%	13
Portugal	1.13%	15
Spain	1.87%	12
Turkey	4.44%	6
UK	9.21%	3
US	41.30%	1
Japan	4.12%	7
Non US NATO	54.58%	
Non US NATO + Japan	58.70%	
Total NATO	95.88%	
Total NATO + Japan	100.00%	

Designed by Bill Yenne
Edited by John Kirk and Bill Yenne

Acknowledgements

We wish to thank Bob Foster of McDonnell Douglas, and Jim Croslin and Mike Hatfield, both of LTV. We also—and especially—wish to thank Master Sergeant Ken Hammond of the US Air Force, who supplied a great many of the photos taken by himself and by his Air Force Audio-Visual Squadron colleagues.

Photo Credits

All photos courtesy of the United States Air Force and the Department of Defense except:
Armee de l'Air 117 (right)
Avions Marcel Dassault Breguet Aviation 116 (left), 116-117, 117 (top)
Bell Helicopter Textron 200-201
Bison Picture Library 23 (all), 26 (top), 31, 142 (left)
Boeing 4-5, 40, 41, 76, 77 (left), 136-137, 153, 174-175, 175
Chaz Bowyer 15 (right), 26 (bottom)
T Sgt Ed Boyce (USAF) 118 (left), 119 (left), 171, 176, 214 (top)
British Aerospace 36-37, 74, 74-75, 103, 110-111, 111 (top), 112, 113 (left), 114 (right), 115, 133, 134, 146 (bottom), 147 (bottom), 154 (bottom), 155 (top), 166 (left), 186, 187, 192, 212-213, 218-219
Bundes der Vert via Defense 29 (top)
MSgt Mike Daniels (USAF) 77 (right), 136 (left), 224
Defense Mapping Agency 179, 193, 209, 215 (base maps only)
© RE DeJauregui 148, 149
Fairchild Republic 79 (right), 96 (upper right), 143 (bottom), 181 (left)
1st Lt Susan L Fielder (USAF) 65
Ford Aerospace & Communications 135
General Dynamics 58, 98 (bottom), 129, 131
SSgt Gus Garcia (USAF) 97
MSgt Ken Hammond (USAF) 51, 59, 71, 81, 110 (left), 120 (left), 122 (left), 157, 160, 170, 177, 202 (left)
Imperial War Museum, London 7
Lockheed 22-23, 32, 34-35, 48 (right), 56, 57, 83 (left), 120 (upper right), 166-167

TSgt Jose Lopez Jr (USAF) 67
LTV 182 (left), 211
McDonnell Douglas 2-3, 10-11, 17 (top), 43, 61, 85, 90-91, 100-101, 105 (top), 106 (left), 121, 124 (left), 125 (top), 126-127, 144, 147 (left and right), 150 (bottom), 151 (all), 158 (bottom), 159 (all), 183, 184-185, 188-189, 190-191, 194-195, 200 (left), 203, 214 (left)
Messerschmitt-Bolkow-Blohm 42, 104-105, 106-107, 108-109, 155 (bottom), 163, 196-197, 197, 204
SSgt Dave Nolan 113 (right), 114 (left)
MSgt Pat Nugent (USAF) 60 (left), 70 (right), 82, 83 (right), 106 (upper right), 122 (right), 123, 124 (center), 172, 173 (right), 202 (right), 210
TSgt James Pearson (USAF) 181 (right)
SSgt Fernando Serna (USAF) 118 (right), 119 (right), 120 (bottom), 164 (all), 165, 205
Swedish Air Force 46-47, 47, 54, 68
TASS News Service 44-45
R Williams / R Ward 29 (bottom)
via R Ward 28, 30, 33
RJ Wilson 27
© Bill Yenne 14-15, 39, 73, 84, 92, 93, 107 (top and right), 138 (all), 139 (left), 142 (top), 146 (top), 150 (top), 154 (top), 179, 180 (top), 198-199
Bill Yenne 179, 193, 209, 215 (battle lines and arrows only)

Overleaf: A US Air Force C-130 Hercules and a Luftwaffe C-160 Transall fly in formation over the American Military Cemetery in Luxembourg—in fitting tribute to, and sobering reminder of, those who have given their lives for their families and friends.

LTG: Luftwaffe Air Transport Wing
MAC: Military Airlift Command (A major US Air Force command)
MF: Marineflieger (West German marine air force)
MFG: Marineflieger Geschwader (West German marine air force wing)
MIDS: NATO Multifunctional Information Distribution System
MOU: Memorandum of Understanding
NADC: NATO Air Defense Committee
NADGE: NATO Air Defense Ground Environment System
NAEW: NATO AEW force
NAFAG: NATO Air Force Armaments Group
NATO: North Atlantic Treaty Organization
NATS: Naval Air Transport Service

NAVSOUTH: Allied Naval Forces Southern Europe
NAVSTAR: US-developed international navigation and global positioning satellite
NIS: NATO Identification System
NICS: NATO Integrated Communications System
NORTHAG: Northern Army Group
NSSMS: NATO Seasparrow Surface Missile System
NST: NATO Staff Targets
ONEATAF: Allied Tactical Air Force, First
PACAF: Pacific Air Forces (A major US Air Force Command—the Pacific equivalent of USAFE)
RAF: Royal Air Force (Great Britain's air force)
RRP: Rapid Reinforcement Plan
Reforger: Return of Forces to Germany—US series of de-

fensive tactical exercises in the Federal Republic of Germany
SAC: Strategic Air Command (A major US Air Force command)
SACEUR: Supreme Allied Commander for Europe
SACLANT: Supreme Allied Commander Atlantic
SHAPE: Supreme Headquarters, Allied Powers, Europe
SIXATAF: Allied Tactical Force, Sixth
SLUF: Short Little Ugly Fellow, aka the A-7 Corsair II tactical aircraft
SNA: Soviet Naval Aviation
SOSTAS: Standoff Surveillance and Target Acquisition System
SRARM: Short-Range Anti-Radiation Missile
STANAG: NATO standardization agreement
STOL: Short Take-off and Landing

TAC: Tactical Air Command (A major US Air Force command)
TFS: Tactical Fighter Squadron (USAF)
TFW: Tactical Fighter Wing (USAF) (Note: Wings contain Squadrons)
TRW: Tactical Reconnaissance Wing
TWOATAF: Allied Tactical Force, Second
UK: the United Kingdom
UKAIR: United Kingdom Air Forces
USAAF: US Army Forces (precursor of the US Air Force)
USAF: US Air Force
USAFE: US Air Forces in Europe
USCINCEUR: US Commander in Chief in Europe
VTOL: Vertical Take-off and Landing
VSTOL: Very Short Take-Off and Landing